Basic Christianity

Addresses

of
D. Elton Trueblood

Edited, and with an
Introduction
by
James R. Newby

RICHMOND, INDIANA

Published by
Friends United Press
101 Quaker Hill Drive
Richmond, IN 47374

L.C. # 78-51839
I.S.B.N. 0-913408-37-9

Printed in the United States of America
by
Prinit Press, Dublin, IN 47335

Contents

2031503

Introduction

The best way to understand the greatness of a people is through the study of their leaders. D. Elton Trueblood is a distinguished leader among his contemporary Christians, and a giant within his own religious society. One way in which we understand why he is such a leader is by reading the addresses he has delivered before gatherings of his religious community. With the publication of these messages, this is now possible. These addresses are arranged to provide the reader with a chronological look at the development of Dr. Trueblood's thought. Through this book we are able to follow the spiritual pilgrimage of a Quaker leader, and also a people, for by learning about the thought of a leader, we invariably learn about the character of that people which he claims as his own.

The Society of Friends is Elton Trueblood's spiritual home. He is by birthright a Friend, being born into a Quaker family near Ackworth, Iowa, on December 12, 1900. His family affiliation with Friends extends back to England where Arnold Trueblood died in prison at Lincoln, in 1658, as a persecuted member of the young religious society. In the Preface to his book, *The People Called Quakers*, Dr. Trueblood writes that he belongs to "an unbroken heritage for which I am not responsible, but for which I am profoundly grateful. . .The Quaker way of life is something with which I have been intimately acquainted from my earliest memories. Very soon, as a small boy, I learned that the heritage in which I was reared was a rich one."[1] This reverent appreciation for his

[1]D. Elton Trueblood, *The People Called Quakers* (New York: Harper and Row, 1966), p. x.

religious roots is one reason why he is such an able spokesman for the Society of Friends.

The life of Elton Trueblood has moved among and interacted with the most influential Quaker leaders of our century. He had a close working relationship with H.G. Wood while at Woodbrooke in England. He came to teach at Haverford one year before Rufus Jones retired, and thus was able to relate to this well known religious thinker as a colleague. He was with Henry Cadbury while a graduate student at Harvard Divinity School, and occupied Professor Cadbury's home while serving as Acting Dean of Harvard Chapel. He worked closely with Alexander Purdy at both Hartford Seminary and the Earlham School of Religion. Douglas Steere was Elton Trueblood's colleague during his tenure at Haverford. Thomas Kelly followed Dr. Trueblood in the department of Philosophy at Haverford, in the summer of 1936. He was with Howard Brinton while teaching in both California and Pennsylvania. He continues to have a close friendship and working relationship with Elfrida Vipont Foulds which has lasted for 38 years, and he was a close friend of President Herbert Hoover, conducting his memorial service in October of 1964. The close personal contact with these Quaker leaders has greatly influenced the life of Elton Trueblood, and no doubt Elton Trueblood's life has influenced theirs.

As a Quaker academician, Dr. Trueblood graduated from one Quaker college, William Penn, and has taught at three others — Guilford, Haverford and Earlham. As a Quaker administrator, he has been on the board of trustees of two Friends colleges, and as a Quaker lecturer he has spoken in all the major yearly meetings in America and also in those of London and East Africa.

Elton Trueblood has traveled among, and has been welcome within all branches of Friends. His book, *The People Called Quakers,* represents a combination of all elements of thought within the Society of Friends, and when published gained immediate acceptance by all major groups. He writes about this specifically Quaker literary effort in his autobiography, *While It Is Day*: "...I made a conscious effort to be fair to all aspects of the Quaker movement. The fact that I had had the opportunity to become acquainted with all the major current brands of Quakerism, on both sides of the Atlantic, made this particular emphasis possible."[2] As we study the life of this man, we soon discover that the history of the Society of Friends is his history. This is the people with whom the Trueblood life moved and is moving, and through whom he is both moulder and moulded.

As this dynamic interworking between individual and religious community developed, certain leadership characteristics emerged. Certain persons are able to rise above others and assume leadership. The reason why some people attain leadership positions has come to the forefront of my thinking as I have compiled this book. As I studied the character of a man who has been on the cutting edge of not only Quaker thought, but much of Christian thought for the past forty years, I have tried to answer this question. I have found it helpful to study the characteristics that are prevalent in a leader's personality. Since this study is specifically concerned with Elton Trueblood, I shall focus my attention on five characteristics that mark the life of this Quaker leader.

In the first place, Dr. Trueblood is a persistent disciplinarian. Once he is stirred by a motive or purpose, there is no quitting. He learned long ago that if something is going to get done, one has to begin and not quit until finished. His writing career has been successful because he has been able to discipline his life to allow for time to begin a book, and then persist in a disciplined fashion until it is completed. The discipline of time is very important to his career, and he often repeats those insightful words of William Penn:

> There is nothing of which we are apt to be so lavish as of time, and about which we ought to be more solicitous; since without it we can do nothing in this world. Time is what we want most, but what, alas! we use worst; and for which God will certainly most strictly reckon with us, when time shall be no more.[3]

In his autobiography Elton Trueblood echoes this sentiment when he writes, "We must use the time which we have because even at best there is never enough."[4] His days are full, beginning at 6:00 A.M. and concluding strictly at 10:00 P.M..

[2]D. Elton Trueblood, *While It Is Day* (New York: Harper and Row, 1974), p. 78.
[3]William Penn, *Some Fruits Of Solitude* (London: Headley Brothers, 1905), p. 16.
[4]*While It Is Day*, p. 67.

which he jokingly calls "Quaker midnight." Within this sixteen hour period, Elton Trueblood can live more fully, and get more done, than most people accomplish in two days.

Secondly, the genius of Elton Trueblood is realized because of his vivid imagination. His mind is agile, for he is always asking questions and developing possible solutions. He is an "idea man." I have never been with Elton when he did not have a new idea to promote which would help ease the burden of a perplexing problem. Throughout his life he has had many wonderful ideas designed to raise the level of human understanding, and point us beyond ourselves. His most recent venture is the realization of a dream which he has fostered for many years. Approximately two years ago the Yokefellow Academy was organized and established in Richmond, Indiana, to educate lay people for ministry. This dream come true focuses all of Trueblood's thinking on lay religion, and puts it into practice through four educational methods: 1) *Tutorials.* Those living within driving distance of the Academy can take advantage of study on a one-to-one basis. This can be done weekly, bi-weekly or monthly. 2) *Correspondence.* For those who live too far from the Academy, work can be done through correspondence. In this manner each can study in his or her home area as interest dictates. 3) *Local Centers.* Additional opportunities are given by the establishment of local centers of the Academy around the country. 4) *Field Work.* Teachers affiliated with the Academy are available for teaching short courses in churches, on college campuses, or in other places where there is sufficient interest.

The premises upon which the Academy is based are two: 1) education is too good to limit to the young, and 2) theology, i.e. knowledge about God, is too important to limit to professionals. The Academy is already making an important contribution to the Christian ministry, and is destined to be a guiding light for hundreds of individuals in the future.

A third leadership characteristic of Elton Trueblood is his interest in small things. To understand this, one need only to watch Elton outside his study as he carefully trims his beautiful rose bushes, or waters his gorgeous bed of tulips. In the mind of this notable Quaker there is no such thing as menial work. All work is important, whether it be writing a book or cutting the grass. The flexibility of Dr. Trueblood to move from one area of labor to another, with no shame whatsoever, is a mark of his eminence.

A fourth characteristic that is easily recognizable in the Trueblood personality is his sense of humor. A good leader knows when to laugh, and Elton can clearly discern the proper moment when a good joke is in order. Many times he has said, "I don't trust the theology of any man who is without a sense of humor." A sample of Dr. Trueblood's wit was recently shared with me at the 1977 May Day Celebration on the campus of Earlham College. As I greeted him, I could tell by the twinkle in his eyes that he was anxious to share his latest anecdote. He began slowly. . ."An advertisement in a local English paper read in part, 'This Sunday the guest lecturer at Christ Church will be Edgar Jones,   A.B., B.D., D.D., Lit. D., LL.D.' " And then with characteristic good timing, he sprung the punch line: " 'Topic ——— *Humility!'* "

His sense of humor does not detract from his profundity, but combines with it to make his message that much more powerful. We can say of Elton Trueblood, as Macaulay said of Addison, that he possesses "a mirth consistent with tender compassion for all that is frail, and with profound reverence for all that is sublime."

The fifth characteristic I shall discuss in this brief introduction, is Elton Trueblood's wholistic view of life. I consider this living model of wholism which he has given generally to Christianity, and specifically to the People Called Quakers, his most important contribution. As one reads these addresses, he immediately senses this dynamic characteristic of the man behind the message. We discover at once that we cannot label Elton Trueblood with the common terms generally employed to box an individual into a certain corner of thought. We soon realize that the labels of "evangelical" or "liberal," "pietist" or "activist," are not suitable when used alone to describe him. He is a combination of all these elements. He is evangelical because he is Christ-centered, and he is liberal in the sense that he is intellectually and spiritually alive. He is concerned about nourishing his inner life through prayer and worship, but he is also actively concerned about his fellow humans and seeks justice for those who are oppressed. In his book, *The New Man For Our Time*, Dr. Trueblood points out the combination needed in this divided Christian world: "The polarization of our time, which produces half men who could be whole men, may be made vivid by reference to both the roots and the fruits of the Christian faith. The pietist is one who stresses chiefly the roots; the activist is one who stresses chiefly the fruits. Service without devotion is rootless; devotion without service is fruitless."[5] In his own life Elton Trueblood stresses both the roots and the fruits, and thus demonstrates in a personal way, the power of Christian wholism.

I began this discussion of the personal characteristics of Elton Trueblood with the question of why certain persons rise to a position of leadership. In the case of this Quaker leader, it is because of his 1) *persistent discipline,* 2) *vivid imagination,* 3) *interest in small things,* 4) *sense of humor,* and 5) *wholistic approach to life.* These five characteristics do not exhaust the qualities present in Elton Trueblood's leadership, but they do help us to see, even in a limited way, why he is such a respected leader.

I cannot share the characteristics of a man without mentioning the major way in which he has used his unique abilities. The name of Elton Trueblood has always been identified with the finest in religious writing. Few authors have remained so consistently at the top of their profession. In spite of a natural talent for writing, Elton Trueblood has worked long and hard to be in the distinguished position he now holds as "dean of American religious writing." Each of his thirty-one volumes displays the kind of hard thinking and careful research for which he has become known. He is a man well acquainted with the classics of religious literature, which continue to keep him in touch with the genius of earlier centuries. In this sense he does not possess a chronological snobbery, which delights in everything that is new and disregards everything that is old. His books reflect a writer who has been able to salvage from the past those important thoughts which can help us in the present.

[5]D. Elton Trueblood, *Tne New Man For Our Time* (New York: Harper and Row, 1979), p. 25.

His aim in writing is excellence in both content and style. He recognizes that novelty of method will not produce good literature, but only studious labor. The writing of D. Elton Trueblood is not an affair of fashion — here today and gone tomorrow. As an author he has obeyed a stronger law than the vagaries of vogue. He has sought to be deaf to the cries of the superficial market of the time, and has chosen instead the direction of quality with a touch of freshness. By so doing he has avoided the trappings of producing literature just for the day, and has instead given us works that will light our paths for years to come.

The life of Elton Trueblood is a combination of events and personality, that when fused produces genius. When a singer listens to a good vocalist something responds and he or she sings a little better. In a like manner, hearing Elton Trueblood speak or reading his thoughtful words, makes people more determined to become better servants of humanity. It is what we bring to the drama of life that counts, and Dr. Trueblood is able to equip us so that we always bring our best. Many times he has said that if we do not live up to our potential, then we are cheating ourselves and humankind. The enthusiasm for life that this intellectual leader possesses is contagious. Always he is calling forth our best, beckoning us to move beyond our self-imposed limits, and dream seemingly impossible dreams.

Elton Trueblood's own dreams are numerous and many have been actualized. He has had many dreams for his beloved religious society, and as we read these addresses they become evident. But there is something more profound at work in these messages than a speculative dreamer. What grabs us, and what lifts off the written page to touch us, is a sense of *hope*. This optimism for the future of the Society of Friends is prevalent throughout these lectures, and offers to us that vision of wholeness that Elton Trueblood has personally realized in himself. He provides in these addresses an introduction to the next period of Quaker history. It is no accident that these addresses begin on a note of "discovery" and conclude with a "vision." Such has been the spiritual progression of the Society of Friends. If George Fox had not first discovered, he would never have had his vision of "a great people to be gathered." The vision presented to us by the leading Quaker spokesman of our day, offers us a combination instead of a separation. To be a Quaker in today's world requires a tough mind and a tender heart, and a sensitivity that will not allow history to repeat itself. The divisions of the past must not become models for the present. Elton Trueblood bids us follow a different drummer who leads us down the path of Quaker wholeness. By following this path we move from separatism to unity, from division to fusion. If we can personally experience the dynamic of wholism, we soon discover, as Elton Trueblood discovered long ago, that this is where the power really lies. In this moving center of activism and pietism, we experience the Living Christ, and a sense of hope leads us forward as we courageously face the future, boldly proclaiming the wholistic message of Quakerism.

At first thought I had intended to call this volume, "The Quaker Addresses of D. Elton Trueblood." Upon further consideration, however, I realized that the appeal of this title was somewhat limited. These essays are of much greater magnitude and deserving of wider distribution than just within the Society of Friends. Quaker books produced only for Quakers are not very important, for I believe, with Dr. Trueblood, that we are living in the post-denominational age. It is my hope and sincere desire to reach seekers of all religious affiliations, and this is why the title *Basic Christianity* was chosen. The recovery of basic Christianity is really what the Society of Friends is all about, for when the People Called Quakers first exploded on the religious scene of Seventeenth Century England, their motivating concern was the revival of primitive Christianity. They believed, in the words of George Fox their founder, "If but one man or woman were raised up by his power, to stand and live in the same spirit, that the Prophets and Apostles were in. . .that man or woman should shake all the country in their profession for ten miles around."

For this volume I have selected eleven addresses out of many. I am not able to include, for instance, Dr. Trueblood's Swarthmore Lecture at London Yearly Meeting in 1939, since it is far too long. I have selected those of a manageable size that were written over many years and delivered at a variety of Quaker gatherings. I had to be conservative in my selection, for the author's works are so voluminous that it would take many volumes of this size to present all of his Quaker addresses. If we isolate the ones chosen in time and place, and identify them too closely with their occasion or circumstance, we shall only misunderstand them. We do best to bring to them not our knowledge of Quakerism, nor our particular theological perspective, but our personal experience of the Christian life.

Samuel Johnson has written, ". . .the vernal flowers, however beautiful and gay, are only intended by nature as preparatives to autumnal fruits" (The Rambler No. 5). This is by no means universally true, but it is true of the life of Elton Trueblood. In this, the autumn of his life, we can see the many marks which he has left on the Society of Friends. Only time will be able to develop those qualities of his influence not yet known. In these, the "Rambler Years" of his earthly pilgrimage, it is a pleasure to make available, in book form, these valuable essays. Although these have already been printed separately, it is not likely that any potential reader possesses a complete set. It is therefore a privilege to present to contemporary readers the present collection of addresses.

Cincinnati, Ohio   — James R. Newby
Summer, 1977

Chapter 1

The Quaker Discovery

It is to me tonight a very sobering and touching fact to realize that it is probably true that there are more persons whom I know and love gathered in this room than have ever been under one roof before. And what I say for myself must be true for almost everybody here. It is not something to take lightly.

The name of Swarthmore is a magic name in the history of Quakerism. The message that we are to talk about tonight, to interpret, came to Swarthmore Hall in England two hundred and eighty-five years ago this summer. On that occasion, George Fox and some of his Friends visited Swarthmore Hall for the first time. And as they did so, that remarkable woman, Margaret Fell, was touched in a most stirring manner. The message came to her, primarily, in the little church, near Swarthmore, when George Fox stood up upon one of the benches and spoke directly to the people. He spoke to them of the necessity of inner experience rather than outward ceremonials. He gave his message directly to the hearts of these people, and said in part: "Art thou a child of Light? And hast thou walked in the Light? And what thou speakest, is it from God?" Margaret Fell has left us her own record of what this did to her. "This affected me so," she said, "that it cut me to the heart, and then I saw clearly we were all wrong, so I sat me down in my pew again, and cried bitterly."

We dare not hope that any one of us here tonight will be cut

This message was delivered at the Friends World Conference, held at Swarthmore, Pennsylvania, in 1937.

to the heart as much as she was, although it would be wonderful if we could be. But, certainly, this message of the Light of Christ, which cut her to the heart, is the same message which Herbert Wood and I shall attempt to present again, as it has been so often presented in these two hundred and eighty-five years.

It is hard for us today to see why this message was so piercing, but piercing it certainly was. And the piercing message usually was a message of the Light. The figure of speech of the light was a figure peculiarly appropriate to the minds of the early Friends. It comes on page after page of their journals and their epistles.

Now this was a figure of speech, and as a figure of speech, it had both its advantages and its disadvantages. Its primary advantage was that it was a matter of poetry, and we can always be more acute about things of the spirit when we speak the language of poetry than we are when we speak the language of strict logic or of scientific method. But it had the disadvantage of all poetry. It was vague and ambiguous and equivocal, and it is not, therefore, surprising that men have made different interpretations of what the Light means. Indeed, these interpretations have gone all the way between two well-known extremes — extremes familiar to every one of us in this room. On the one hand, there is the Calvinist extreme, with all the dangers of the Calvinist heresy, emphasizing the notion that the Light is something utterly alien to our human spirit; and on the other hand, it has been interpreted as mere humanism, maintaining that it is the light of human nature, or the light of reason.

We do well to be afraid of both of these extremes, as we do in almost any great question of the human spirit. Certainly, the extreme of humanism is a dangerous one, because it is clear historically that unless our faith is in God, who is more than we are, a genuine Father of our spirit, our religion becomes sentimental, weak, and powerless. And it is clear that the early Friends were not speaking merely of the inner light in them. Their characteristic expression was, "The Light of Christ." This you find stated by William Penn. You often find simply the words, "The Light."

Now, today we are in a position to take seriously this figure of the Light. We happen to know a great deal more about light than Friends did many generations ago, and it is one of those figures of speech, which, instead of becoming out of date, has become more valuable with the changes of human thought and experience.

It is certainly one of the oldest figures of speech in the world. I went a few days ago into a concordance to see how many times this figure of the light, meaning not physical light, but the light in the heart, appeared in the Bible. You will all notice, if you try the same experiment, that it happens literally dozens of times, appearing about an equal number of times both in the Old Testament and in the New. It has appeared in subsequent religious literature. There is something about it wonderfully appropriate to the human spirit. And for that reason we are wise to take it seriously. And what I want to do tonight is to take it seriously to see what this figure, which devout men have loved, really means if we try to understand Light as our intelligence of today has shown it to us.

One thing we quickly discover is this, that this old controversy, which, by the way, has more than once rent the Society of Friends, this old controversy concerning whether the Light is an inner light or outer light, is one which is overcome by a deeper understanding and appreciation of the figure itself.

In physical life, is the light inner, or is the light outer? Those are both meaningless terms, as we see in the case of electric light. You must have the bulb, which is the medium, but you must have the energy coming from the electric wires.

Where does the light come from? Who knows? And to call it electricity is only to use a name for a mystery. It is a mystery. It is neither inner nor outer. It is, as George Fox said, simply light in the absolute sense. All that we know in our humble state is some of the ways in which light appears.

Now, in modern physical science, men are still arguing concerning the nature of light, theoretically. There are still some who maintain it is fundamentally undulatory, others who maintain that it is fundamentally corpuscular, and they do not agree. But this much is clear, that men have learned the ways in which light appears.

Now, in characteristic modern discoveries, light appears not primarily in the use of wires as it once did, but in the use of various gases as the medium. We find that by using different gases, the same electrical energy can give us light with many different characteristics. Thus, we all see on the streets every night the Neon lamps. The medium there is the Neon gas, which fills the long tubes which make the letters.

Now we have these magnificent sodium lamps. Any of you who have seen the new bridge across the Bay at San Francisco will know how thrilling it is to see the lines of sodium lamps stretching across that great body of water.

But the most remarkable discovery of a medium for light is the use of mercury. Now mercury has long been known as a medium for light, but just in the last few months there has appeared a lamp of almost incredible brilliance. I know most of you have seen accounts of this lamp in the newspaper and in the journals. Like you, I read of these accounts, the accounts of a lamp which would make an intrinsic brilliance greater than that of the sun, of a lamp that would be equal to hundreds and hundreds of lamps like those in this room, of a lamp which by itself would make more than enough light for this large Field House, or any other such large building.

And so I made a trip, when I knew I had this address to give, and I was trying to learn all I could, to the inventor of this remarkable instrument, and I told him I would like to see it, and to my utter amazement he said: "You may see it if you wish," and he pulled one out of his vest pocket, and showed it to me. I had certainly supposed it would be as big as this desk, and here it was, a tiny thing, about the size of a safety match. I asked him if he would let me have one, because I thought people would like to see one. I realize that most of you cannot see it, but some of you can. I am holding one in my hand at this moment. It is a bit of quartz. The quartz has inside of it a small cavity, a cylindrical cavity, which is chiefly a vacuum, and the whole thing inside is about the size of an ordinary sewing needle. And in this vacuum between the electrodes is a small amount of mercury, perhaps equal to an ordinary drop of water.

This bulb is made of ordinary quartz, and ordinary mercury. There are electrodes at the ends. And when this becomes connected with electric power, the electrodes heat that

4

mercury inside and, because the cavity is so small, it comes to have an almost unbelievable pressure, a pressure of at least fourteen atmospheres under ordinary circumstances. And this terrific pressure gives out this incredibly brilliant light, of which I have spoken, of which you have read.

As I went away from this man's home, you can imagine the wonder and humility and mystery in my own mind. I went saying to myself: "Perhaps the world has been all wrong in its emphasis on big things. Perhaps, things do not have to be big in order to be brilliant and luminous," for he told me that his greatest discovery and the secret of his success lay in the fact that he was willing to make it small.

I think you will be glad to know that five hundred of these bulbs are now being used in the Paris Exposition this summer to light their grounds at night. I suppose the time will come when it will have a very wide use in our modern world.

I said to myself: "What wonderful things might yet come if somehow in the realm of the spirit we could be as wise as this clever man has been?" I wish I had more time to tell you tonight about him, a most remarkable person.

He is a Hollander, a man who has six boys, and who has come to this country because he so feared conscription in Europe. He has settled down in the peace of our land to carry on his physical researches. I went on asking him, later, more about his success, because I wanted to see whether this figure would be meaningful for you and me, and for the Society of Friends, who were first called the Children of the Light. He said that after he learned to make this bulb small, he needed two things. First, he needed to have a medium of great intensity. And second, he had needed a way of carrying off the excess energy so that it would not burst the capillary tube. The intensity was achieved by making the cavity small, and using heavy quartz about it. And the second qualification was achieved by putting around this a small circulating tube of water, so that the light is cold light as it goes out, and the excess energy is thus carried away.

So I said to myself: "I wonder if we might have these conditions, because certainly there are conditions for the emergence of light in the human spirit." What Friends did in the middle of the seventeenth century was not really to

5

enunciate a new theory of the light. They were not philosophers of the light, but children of the Light. They gave no new conception either of the nature of man or the nature of God. They gave, really, no new doctrine. They did emphasize the reality of direct experience of God. They did say over and over again that Christ has come to teach His people that He can be known at firsthand, here and now. They maintain it is possible to have knowledge, not in the sense of description, but in the sense of acquaintance. But all of this is old. For generations men have told about the possibility of the direct knowledge of God, and of the direct presence of Christ in their hearts.

But what was the Quaker discovery, if it was a discovery? My friends, was it not this, that they discovered some of the conditions under which the light appears, as Cornelius Bol has discovered the conditions under which the brilliance like that of sunlight appears? He has not made it, and they did not make it, but they found out the way in which it comes.

As I read the journals of the 17th century Friends, this is what impressed me most, that they were almost supernaturally sensitive in their spirits, that they were genuinely illuminated, that they were genuinely able to see far ahead of their time various social evils, such as that of war. It is almost incredible. We know how William James, in his *Varieties of Religious Experience*, has as an outsider given the weight of his authority to this fact, that Friends, generations before others, were sensitive to these things. They were genuinely illuminated. The light actually shone.

When we talk about the Light, we are, therefore, talking not about a doctrine, we are talking about a fact of history, a fact of history which reminds us of the coming of Christ in Palestine. They were convinced that this Light which they knew, which illumined their consciences, was the same Light which was genuinely incarnated in Jesus Christ. And that seemed to be why they called it the Light of Christ.

Do you see how their experience had something in common with that of St. John? In St. John's gospel, he was trying to show the relationship between the revelations of God at different times. He, however, was at the focal point of history, at which time Christ came. His task was to relate the Light of

Christ then with what had come before, and so he said: "The Light that came long ago is the same Light that is come now, fully in Christ."

That, of course, is what we find in the first chapter of John.

Now, the Friends of the 17th century were also relating the revelations of God, only they were beginning with the experience of the historic Jesus, and they said: "This Light that we know is the same Light that appeared in Him." You see what a similar kind of connection it is, except that St. John reasoned from what was then present to a former time, from Christ backward, and the early Friends reasoned and connected from themselves backward to Christ. They found that it was the same Light. And all that they had learned was the way in which it comes.

Now, first as to the intensity. They discovered that the most intense medium for them was a situation of worship in which men learned how to be quiet, and this quietness was not merely a cessation from words, not merely a cessation from action, but indeed a quietness of the whole mind and spirit. And above all, it was a quietness in which they came together as a group to be still and to listen. And this made one of the most intense moods that men know.

Do you see how similar it is to what must happen in the inside of this little capillary tube when this mercury vapor becomes perfectly diffused over the little space, filling it — no wheels moving, no noise, perfectly still as far as the eye can see, but wonderfully intent.

That is what happens in Friends' meetings. It is certainly a great misunderstanding of what happens at worship to suppose it is quietness. As a matter of fact, as many of us in this room can attest, the characteristic experience is one of the most intense spiritual experiences, and sometimes one of the most rapid mental quickenings. I may humbly speak of my own experience in this regard, which, I am sure, is like yours. Often in sitting in a genuine meeting for worship, my mind works more rapidly than it ever does at any other time or work. I will think of a whole speech sometimes in a few minutes. There will come together in my mind a bit of poetry I learned long ago, a phrase from the Bible, an illustration from modern science, a quotation from a classical author — all of these so different in themselves, but they coalesce in my mind and become a new unity. Does not that happen also to you?

It is one of the real contributions of our late Friend, John William Graham, that he has told us that the meeting for worship is really the workshop of the minister, the place in which the various chips of lumber come together in a new piece that the world has not seen before. As a matter of fact, this is precisely what happens in poetic composition.

John Livingston Lowes has done us all a service in reconstructing what happened in the mind of Samuel Taylor Coleridge, as he has shown us in *The Road to Xanadu*. He has shown how in the *Ancient Mariner* Coleridge used phrases, of the origin of which he was perhaps even himself unconscious, but in a high moment of poetic inspiration they came together in a new unity. Wordsworth says in an almost hackneyed and benign phrase that "poetry is emotion recollected in tranquility." You know it as an intense tranquility, but you call it "quietism" and miss the point entirely.

Perhaps, the greatest contribution that Friends have made is to show men everywhere this intense meaning, not that it is the origin of light — God forbid that we might say so — but that there is that in us which we may humbly say is the medium through which illumination to men can come. This intense medium can use the common clay of our humanity. It uses the ordinary mercury, such as we have in the thermometer, the ordinary quartz, and the ordinary wires. What men learned in the middle of the 17th century, as indeed all Christians have known, was that the ordinary work-a-day men, like the fishermen, who were the first Disciples, might become centers of illumination through the love of God.

The second of these important necessities is that, in the case of the mercury lamp, there shall be some way of carrying off the excess energy. There is always a subtle danger that our experience shall be ingrowing, that we shall luxuriate in our Christian experience, that we shall associate always with those who feel as we do, reassuring one another in our deepest convictions. And this can become a matter of self-indulgence. Unless we have some way in which the light that is in us can be carried off, in which the energy thus released can go out, the capillary tube will be burst. That has been the experience of those groups that were merely the representatives of what was once called "enthusiasm."

Where are now the Muggletonians, for example? They used phrases like those of Friends, but Muggleton now is only a name.

Friends have early learned how to carry over the light into the making of a better world, into the freeing of slaves, into the releasing of the conditions of captivity of every kind, into the helping of the Indians, into the improvement of the conditions of the prisons, as Elizabeth Fry has done which Janet Whitney has so shown us in her lovely book.

Friends have learned this second secret, that the light must be spread and diffused, and the energy carried off, else it will burst in the very light it is making.

The sensitiveness of spirit is something that can be lost, and if our religion is self-indulgent, we shall lose it. We all know how we can lose sensitiveness in other realms. You know the sad passage from Charles Darwin in which he tells how he lost sensitiveness to music. There have surely been people who have lost even the kind of sensitiveness Friends have. We could lose it now. That is why we all feel so keenly, as we must, about our meeting for worship. That is the capillary tube on the one hand. We must have the Service Committee, and our foreign work for the Indians and the colored people — all of these out-going things compose the other side of our life. And this keeps us sane, and above all, it keeps the illumination real.

If I may say a personal word — many of you have asked me why I should be willing to leave a charming place like Haverford College, steeped in the Quaker tradition, and go three thousand miles away to a secular university like Leland Stanford. I can only say to these people that I think I do it because it is the Quaker way. It is not the Quaker way, if we have a message, to keep it among ourselves. We dare not go on merely saving the already saved, and convincing the already convinced.

We must have our places in which we keep in our own lives and increase our own illumination, but that illumination we lose unless every one of us, in his way, is an evangelist. Our evangelism is along different lines because we have different vocations. It is the vocation of some to carry it through the

Service Committee to the miners of the West Virginia region. It is the vocation of some to carry it into great international centers, like those of Geneva, Berlin, and Vienna. It is the vocation of some to carry it to their neighbors, as they are farming, and carrying on business. It is the vocation of some to carry it to our academic centers. But carry it we must, else we lose it?

Before coming here, I gave my manuscript for tonight to our common friend, Augustus Murray, a man who has been very sorry that he could not come. Scarcely anybody hates to miss this meeting as much as he does. And he returned my manuscript with this lovely little thought — two verses from Whittier — perfectly appropriate to this speech:

> Only in the gathered silence
> Of a calm and waiting frame,
> Light and wisdom as from Heaven
> To the seeker came.
>
> Not to ease and aimless quiet
> Doth that inward answer tend,
> But to works of love and duty,
> As our being's end.

Those two verses have it all — the intense quietness of the intense quiet that releases the Light, and the outer actions of love and duty that keep our sensitive spirits keen, so that the Light of Christ may not be lost to it.

The Light of Christ is not of our making. The Light of Christ comes from the love of God. But the mystery, which is from the beginning, is this, that this Light of Christ, who is incarnate Jesus of Nazareth, may also shine in our feeble hearts, if we fulfill the conditions under which it appears.

Chapter 2

A Radical Experiment

Something has gone wrong in the modern world. Men and women, who are the heirs of all the ages, standing at the apex of civilization, as thus far achieved, are a confused and bewildered generation. This is not true merely of the vanquished, but of a majority of the victors. It is true, not merely of those who live in the cellars of bombed houses and ride in converted cattle cars; it is true likewise of those who live in steam-heated apartments and ride in Pullman drawing rooms.

This is not merely the old story of human sorrow or even the old story of human sin. Both of these we expect, and both of these we have, but even the most optimistic person is bound to note that today we have something else in addition to these. We have something very similar to the loss of nerve, so convincingly portrayed by Gilbert Murray and other analysts of the decline of Hellenic culture. The ancient loss of nerve we can understand, because of the flagrant inadequacies of the pagan faith, but the present failure of spirit is more difficult to understand; it has occurred in the heart of Christendom.

One of the major symptoms of our spiritual decline is the relative absence of joy. This is understandable in a country like Germany, which is defeated, impoverished and ashamed, but it is noticeable in Anglo-Saxon countries as well. Lacking the overflowing joy of unified lives, our modern divided and anxious personalities strive desperately and pathetically for

This address was presented as the William Penn Lecture at the sessions of Philadelphia Yearly Meeting, in April of 1947.

11

happiness. Lacking the real thing, we turn to substitutes. The continual demand for exhibitionist photographs in the popular magazines is an evidence, not of vigorous love between men and women, but of its absence. Our worst troubles, as so much of modern medicine testifies, arise primarily from psychological rather than purely physiological sources. The difficulties of modern woman, for example, some of which were almost unknown in earlier generations, have come, not from any physiological alterations in the human stock, but from unwillingness to accept major responsibilities, and from egoistic strivings after success which undermine the basis of real peace of mind.

The upshot of most careful analysis is that the central trouble is in our inner lives rather than our outer condition. The modern world is admittedly perplexing, but, with a sufficiently vibrant faith men could live as joyously and victoriously in it as in any other. In fact, they might live in a better way than mankind ever lived in all preceding centuries. But before there can be a good life at all, modern man must become possessed by a faith sufficient to sustain his life in these troubled times. Such a faith might be an old faith *recovered* or a new faith *discovered*, but one or the other we must have.

Because western man has largely failed either to recover or to discover a vibrant faith, he is perishing. Millions are fatalistic. They feel utterly powerless in the presence of forces which they can neither understand nor control. In spite of our proud achievements, including many in the various arts, there is a widespread sense that we are waiting for a *catastrophe*. If we are capitalists we blame labor, if we are in organized labor we blame the capitalists, and, whoever we are, we blame the government. Meanwhile we sit back and have a drink or some other form of escape. We cultivate more and more the sensual arts, thereby enabling our minds to be free, for a little while, from the haunting sense of insecurity and bewilderment. If the advertisements in the popular magazines are reliable indications, we care supremely about three things — whiskey, perfume, and motor cars.

Life in the west seems to be marked equally by a clear understanding of what man needs and by a tragic inability to provide him with it. Where will men find a faith to sustain and invigorate them in these troubled days? In the Rotary Club? In the Labor Union? In the Farm Bureau? In Eastern mysticism? In national pride? In Free Masonry? In natural science? Not very likely! All of these have their place in human experience and all are capable of producing some spiritual resources, but, both separately and together, they are insufficient. They may serve as temporary substitutes for a living faith, but they cannot succeed in *providing* such a faith. It was not these or anything very much like them which brought the amazing recovery of spirit which occurred in the Greek and Roman world at the beginning of our era.

Most minds turn spontaneously to the church when the paramount problem of spiritual renewal is introduced. Isn't the church in that business? If it is a living faith that we need, let us turn to the church as the one institution which is dedicated exclusively to the perpetuation and promulgation of a saving faith. But here we are as bewildered as anywhere else. The trouble is that so many in the modern world have grave misgivings concerning the ability of the church to provide a saving vision. There is a deep-seated conviction among our neighbors that the experts don't know, any better than do the amateurs, how the job is to be done. Thousands think of churches as stuffy places, concerned with respectability and the conventions, but with no conceivable part in the creation of courage and adventure and joy. Many of those who thus judge the church from the outside are both incorrect and uncharitable in their judgments, but there is, in what they say, enough truth to make their judgment profoundly disquieting.

How disquieting the situation is may be shown in a recent pertinent illustration. A prominent physicist, long head of his department in a well-known American university, recently did some hard thinking on the problem of spiritual reconstruction. He came, finally, to two important conclusions:

a.   We cannot have a decent world merely by scientific endeavor. In addition we must have deep moral convictions and a living religion to sustain them.

b.   There can be no living religion without a fellowship. Because mere individual religion is parasitical, there must be a church or something like it, and people who

13

care about the fate of our civilization will join it.

With these conclusions in mind the physicist set out to attend church in the town where his research was going forward. The first attempt was disappointing, so he tried another kind of church the next Sunday, but it was equally disappointing. He had gone with high hopes and after rigorous thought, but of course his fellow worshippers could not know that this was the case. It seemed to him that these people were merely going through the motions, that they did not mean what they said, that the gospel was to them an old record, worn smooth with much playing. Here, said the physicist, was a world on the very brink of a new hell, and these people had no sense of urgency or of power. The scientist had hoped that at least the sermons would speak to his condition, but they did not. Both seemed trivial.

Here is a scene all too representative of our time. The hungry sheep look up and are not fed. But where would you have sent the physicist with confidence? Where can the requisite vision be found? We can convince the seeker's reason that mere individual religion is insufficient, and that a fellowship is required for the maintenance of man's spiritual structure; but the *ecclesia* to which he turns so hopefully may turn out to be disappointingly *ersatz*. The "sacred fellowship" may be so taken up with struggles for institutional prestige and personal power that the honest seeker is disgusted. There is no denying that many of the best people are outside the churches precisely because they *are* the best people. The fact that they have been disgusted is something in their favor; at least it shows that their standards are encouragingly high.

In the western world there are two main alternatives presented to the average seeker, Protestantism and Catholicism. *The tragedy is that millions find satisfaction in neither.* The evidence for this observation is provided in numerous ways, one of these being the remarkable growth of new cults and movements. Though Protestantism is still the dominant form of Christianity in Anglo-Saxon and Scandinavian countries, it is easy to see why the man who has at least seen the folly of his paganism may not be attracted. The two great evils of Protestantism are that it is *divisive* and that much of it is *insipid.* A man who, having felt the awful

14

crisis in the spirit of man, is seeking the bread of life, too often listens to discussions of the every-member canvass. There are thousands of wonderful and brave men in the Protestant ministry, but far too many of them are practically forced by the organizational system to be promoters or business managers.

If Protestantism is uninviting to the average seekers, Catholicism is equally so. Though there have been some highly publicized conversions of former pagans to the Roman Church, this does not mean that the modern seeker is finding his answer in that quarter. The Roman Catholic Church is repellent to millions of moderns because of its exclusiveness and because of its bias toward totalitarianism. The thoughtful seeker looks at Spain and sees religious totalitarianism in practice. He knows that the Catholic Church does not really believe in freedom of worship. But freedom of worship seems of cardinal importance to the modern seeker who is acutely conscious that truth is complex and that the whole truth is not likely to be contained in any one institution. *Nobody has all the keys there are.*

Where then shall the seeker turn? He knows that both Catholicism and Protestantism include vigorous remnants, particularly among the neo-Thomists on the one hand and the neo-Reformation theologians on the other. But this is theology, and the seeker is looking for something else. He is looking for what the late William James so happily termed, "A Religion of Veracity, rooted in spiritual inwardness." In short, modern man is looking and longing for a New Reformation. He is looking for some new way in which the Eternal Spirit can be incarnated in a living fellowship in this our troubled day. He longs to see more light break forth from God's word.

Great numbers of observers in the western world give assent to every step in our reasoning up to this point, but here they diverge. This is the real crossroads in the thinking of our time. Some believe that the saving faith can come by a revitalization of the Christian gospel, but there are many others who, with equal sincerity and seriousness, do not believe that this is possible. A brilliant exponent of this latter conclusion is Harold Laski. Harold Laski agrees that apart from an inspiring faith we shall perish; he understands perfectly that the Christian gospel performed this function in the ancient world; but he holds that the Christian faith can do so no longer. The old fires, he thinks, are burnt out. His evidence for his conclusion, similar to that already mentioned, is profoundly disquieting. He says that we must have a new faith for the new day, and this he finds emerging from Russia, very much as long ago a new faith emerged from Palestine, the land of his fathers. What Laski dares to say openly is undoubtedly the real conviction of many others, including some who still pay lip service to the Christian world view. His is, of course, the flaming and avowed faith of millions in Europe and Asia who believe that they have found a live alternative to the faith at the basis of western civilization.

There are many pertinent answers which might be given to Mr. Laski. One answer is that there is convincing reason to believe that the Christian gospel is *true* and not merely *useful,* its very effectiveness in the classic culture arising from its essential truth. What is objectively true at one time is equally true at another. If the Living God really *is* like Christ, that is a truth so paramount that changing patterns of culture make very little difference. Actually, of course, the essential human problem has not greatly changed in these centuries. A second answer to Mr. Laski is the historical observation that Christianity has demonstrated a remarkable ability to revive itself from within, by unflinching self-criticism. There have been many ages of revival and ours might be one of them. What has been, *can* be. Important as these two answers are, the most convincing answer would be a contemporary *demonstration.* We cannot revive the faith by argument, but we might catch the imagination of puzzled men and women by an exhibition of a Christian fellowship so intensely alive that every thoughtful person would be forced to respect it. The creation of such a fellowship is the argument that can count in the confused world of our day. If again there appears a fellowship of men and women who show, by their vitality and moral sensitivity and overwhelming joy, that they have found something so real that they no longer seek means of escape, the seekers will have something to join without disappointment and without embarrassment. If there should emerge in our day such a fellowship, wholly without artificiality and free from the dead hand of the past, it would be an exciting event of momentous importance. A society of loving souls without self-seeking struggle for personal prestige or any unreality would be something unutterably precious. A wise person would travel any distance to join it.

It is such a demonstration that is now required. We do not require any new denomination. To start a new denomination of like-minded people is conspicuously easy, but such an enterprise is almost entirely worthless. It is the whole lump that must be leavened, and the leaven cannot be efficacious unless it stays in close connection with the lump. There are several historical examples of such leavening fellowships, the work of St. Francis being one of the best. But how can its counterpart be produced now?

The way in which a humble yet leavening fellowship may be created and guided is a question of the utmost difficulty as it is a question of the utmost importance. It is far more difficult than are most scientific problems, because it deals with more imponderables. In short, wisdom in this field, like wisdom in any *important* field, can come only by a remarkable combination of careful intelligence and creative imagination. It is this to which we should now give our nights and days, and to which we *shall* give our nights and days if we care greatly about the fate of the human race at this juncture. The result might be something radically different from anything we now know.

It is good to remember that the revolutionary fellowship of which we read in the New Testament was a result of careful thought and much disciplined dreaming. In one sense the entire burst of new life was seen as the work of God, a sheer gift of divine grace, but in another sense the work and thought of dedicated men and women were required. In any case, St. Paul and others actually put enormous effort into the problem. His inspired Epistles are given over very largely to his own creative thought about what the nature of a redeeming fellowship might be. In letter after letter the same criteria appear. The fellowship must be marked by mutual affection of the members, by a sense of real equality in spite of difference of function, by inner peace in the face of the world's turmoil and by an almost boisterous joy. The members are to be filled, not

17

with the intoxication of win, but with that of the Spirit. Such people could hardly avoid, as the sequence in the fifth chapter of Ephesians suggests, breaking out in psalms and hymns. In the early Christian community the people sang, not from convention, but from a joy which overflowed. Life was for these people no longer a problem to be solved, but a thing of glory.

We are so hardened to the story that it is easy for us to forget how explosive and truly revolutionary the Christian faith was in the ancient Mediterranean world. The church at first had no buildings, no separated clergy, no set ritual, no bishops, no pope, yet it succeeded in turning life upside down for millions of unknown men and women, giving them a new sense of life's meaning, and superb courage in the face of persecution or sorrow. It is our tragedy that we are living in a day when much of this primal force is spent. Our temper is so different that we hardly understand what the New Testament writers are saying. Once a church was a brave and revolutionary fellowship, changing the course of history by the introduction of discordant ideas; today a church is a place where people go and sit on comfortable benches, waiting patiently until time to go home to their Sunday dinners.

One of the most hopeful signs of our time is that we are beginning to sense the wide disparity between what the church is and what it might be. This point is forced upon us both by contrast with early Christianity and by reference to the unmet needs incident to the crisis of our time. And always the most vigorous critics of the church are those on the inside, who love her. The worst that the outside critics ever say is more than matched by what the devout Christians say. The theological seminaries from coast to coast are filled with impatient young men, eager for internal revolution. Fortunately they are being brought together and given an effective voice in the Interseminary Movement which is producing a set of volumes on the point at issue and which will hold a gathering of about a thousand picked seminarians this summer.

It is good to see the evidence that Christians are already at work in this task of creative dreaming on the question of what a truly redemptive fellowship might be. New movements have been started already, both within the churches and outside

18

them. For the most part, however, the people in these movements are separated from those in other and similar movements, with little sense of sharing in a worldwide enterprise. Some are lonely thinkers, almost unaware that others have had their same impatience with what is offered and the same high vision of what might be accomplished. Others are unaware of similar experiments which have occurred in the past, experiments from which they might learn in planning their contemporary efforts. Success will not come except as we help each other.

Because the task before us has many elements in common with the task of architecture, it is relevant at this point to meditate upon the undoubted success of the modern architectural revival. Our contemporary architectural tendencies constitute one of the clearest evidences of cultural improvement in our generation. We have done very badly in other ways, but we have done remarkably well in this. Modern towns and cities are still ugly, for the most part, but those sections in which contemporary architects, from the recognized schools, have had a free hand, are often very beautiful indeed. Few can fail to be impressed, for example, with the architectural advance shown in Cleveland, whether in the Terminal Tower and its vicinity or in Shaker Square. Equally encouraging is the domestic architecture of the English Garden Cities, of the northern suburbs of Baltimore, and of many communities.

What has been the secret of this new burst of life in the art of building? In every case the gain has come by a delicate combination of appreciation of past models, plus the boldness of real adventure. The boldness alone tends to produce the merely bizarre, while exclusive attention to past models produces the merely quaint, but the combination of the two may be genuinely creative. Dreaming *in vacuo* is usually not very profitable, but dreaming as an imaginative extension of known experience may be extremely profitable.

If we apply this formula to our creative dreaming about what the church might be and ought to be, we get something like the following. We should note with care the principles which made the Christian fellowship so powerful in Philippi and Corinth and Ephesus; we should try to distinguish

19

between the factors of enduring importance and those of local or transitory significance; we should do the same for the Franciscan Movement in the thirteenth century, the Quaker Movement in the seventeenth century, and so on with many more. If these turn out to have some factors in common, in spite of diversity of setting, such factors must be studied with unusual care. At the same time we must rid our minds of most current conceptions about what a church should be in order to try to see what the real needs of men are. Perhaps there ought not to be any distinction at all between clergy and laity; perhaps the life of the church could function better without the ownership of buildings or any property. Many of the early Christian groups met in homes and several met in caves, while some of the seventeenth century Quaker meetings were held in prison. Perhaps real membership should be rigorously restricted to the deeply convinced; perhaps the normal unit should be the small cell rather than the large gathering. Many churches would be ten times as influential if their membership were half as great.

This list of suggestions could be enlarged. It *will* be enlarged by any group of people who try to put into this question the same bold thinking that our best scientists have already put into the questions which they have been so extraordinarily successful in answering, and the same disciplined imagination that our best architects have put into new buildings.

We do not know what the church of the future ought to be, but we can be reasonably sure that it ought to be very different from the church as we know it today. "If something radical is to happen to society," says Dr. Oldham, "something radical must happen to the church." We are due for great changes and we must not resist them. Far from that, we must help to produce them. *No civilization is possible without adventure, and the adventure which our time demands is adventure in the formation of faith-producing fellowships.*

II

In the light of the paramount problem of spiritual reconstruction in our day the Quaker Movement suddenly takes on new significance. What if the Quaker Movement, for all its modesty and smallness, could give some lead to modern seekers, looking for light on what a redemptive fellowship should be or could be? All the effort that has gone into Quakerism would thus become worthwhile. Quakerism would not be an end in itself, but would be one means to a large and glorious end.

What is suggested is a new way of studying the history of the Quaker Movement. We should study it, not for its own sake as an inherited tradition, but in order to see what features of it may wisely be incorporated in the new society that is struggling to emerge from the church we now know. Quaker history as mere antiquarianism is very small business. It is about on a level, spiritually, with genealogy, the least profitable form of literature as well as the most snobbish. Quaker history can be examined, not for the sake of ancestor worship, and not as a contribution to sectarian pride, but as an objective analysis of what all men everywhere can learn from one particular experiment of considerable duration.

The word "experimental" was one of the favorite words of seventeenth century Quakers, partly, no doubt, because of the growing scientific temper of their time. "This I knew experimentally," said Fox, of his fundamental insight which came to him three hundred years ago this year. Though the word "experimentally," in this context, means almost the same as "experientially," it came to be used in the thought and writing of William Penn in our modern laboratory sense. Thus, as is well known, the deepest meaning of the Pennsylvania Colony in the judgment of its founder, was that it constituted an "holy experiment." The principles so highly valued were put to the test where all might see whether they would really work in practical experience.

If we begin to think of the entire Quaker enterprise as one continuous experiment, lasting now for three centuries, we find that this conception is more satisfactory than are the other possible interpretations with which we have been familiar. The idea of experiment provides a particularly happy answer to the moot question of the relation of Quakerdom to the Christian faith and the Christian Church. The most common answers to this question in the past have been four, as follows:

(1) The Society of Friends is what the Christian Church would be if rightly guided.

(2) The Society of Friends is one denomination among others, each of which has its valid contribution to make.

(3) The Society of Friends is not a Christian body, but involves the mysticism of the East as well.

(4) The Society of Friends is a philanthropic body concerned chiefly with the relief of suffering.

The third and fourth of these conceptions have not been held by very many within the Society of Friends, though they have often been held by outsiders. The fourth is a failure to understand the deep religious roots from which good works spring, while the third is a failure to recognize the degree to which the unique events connected with the historic Christian revelation have been stressed by most of the characteristic Quaker thinkers from the beginning.

Most members of the Society of Friends have held either (1) or (2) of the four propositions given above, the earlier generations leaning toward (1) and the later generations toward (2). Neither, however, is wholly satisfactory. The difficulty with the first formulation is that it appears to be lacking in a graceful humility. The trouble with the second formulation is that it appears to be so modest and tolerant that it is almost innocuous. This suggests that both formulations involve important insights but that each is insufficient and that, consequently, it would be desirable to combine them if that were possible. Now the merit of the experimental formula is that it *does* combine them. If we are asked what the experiment is *in*, we must answer that it is *an experiment in radical Christianity*. This keeps the vigor which mutually tolerant denominationalism lacks, but it also keeps the desired humility, in that we point to an experiment and not to a wholly accomplished demonstration. Furthermore, there may be other experiments which can go on concurrently and with great mutual gain.

One of the notable merits of the experimental conception is that it makes impossible a retired and complacent sectarianism. Friends have been guilty of this at various periods, but fortunately we have seldom been entirely lacking in forces of criticism which have sought to destroy such complacency. If ours is an experiment, then it continues, not for our sakes, but for the sake of the entire Church and for the sake of mankind. The experiment is made in the hope that lessons may thereby be learned for the use of all devout men much as an experimental farm produces lessons for all intelligent farmers.

This means that no part of Quaker life is *private*. Friends have sometimes allowed themselves to refer to their schools as "private schools," but this expression is rapidly coming to be seen as a mistake. Such language suggests an ingrown and self-satisfied minority, providing superior privileges for its own children. Quaker schools, if they are true to the major conception, are *public* schools in the sense that they bear a responsibility to the public good, but public schools differently financed and directed than those which are tax-supported.

This means that *Quakerism, when its true vocation is followed, is at once both supremely narrow and supremely ecumenical.* It is narrow in that it makes strict requirements; it is ecumenical in that it exists for the sake of the revivication of the entire Body of Christ. Quakers have failed in their vocation whenever they have descended to the level of one sect among others or when they have intimated that those outside their circle were not Christians. The experimental idea provides an escape from this dilemma.

It cannot be too clearly stated that what early Friends intended was a truly *radical* experiment. George Fox proposed to cut straight through all the religious red tape. If anything seemed artificial and unnecessary, the young shoemaker's apprentice determined to dispense with it, no matter how precious it might have been at other times or how glorified by tradition. Naked reality was what he sought. It is to this that William James was referring when he said, "The Quaker religion is something which it is impossible to overpraise. In a day of shams, it was a religion of veracity rooted in spiritual inwardness and a return to something more like the original gospel truth than men had ever known in England."

George Fox was not a learned man and knew very little about Christian history between the first and seventeenth centuries, but he did know the difference between essentials and non-essentials. Consequently he paid no real attention either to sacraments and liturgical forms made impressive by long usage, or to a priesthood claiming apostolic authority by a succession secured through episcopal ordination. Much as Doctor Johnson later "refuted" Bishop Berkeley by kicking a stone, Fox refuted the sacerdotalists by the direct appeal to experience. He *saw* unordained men and even women ministering with apostolic power. What other evidence could be required?

Though Fox did not claim to know the fine points of the theory of ordination and apostolic succession, he did know that men might be perfectly regular on these points and yet grossly lacking in the evidence either of love of the brethren or of closeness to God. He was aware that men might cling to these externals of the faith when the life had departed from them. He saw that men could easily be meticulous about these matters or even about dogmatic formulations of faith and yet be careless about the weightier matters of mercy, justice and truth. What did he care about the external credentials of the "true church" when he knew in his own soul the kind of illumination that placed him in the order of prophets and apostles? What he proposed, quite simply, was an experiment in veracity.

The experiment has been useful chiefly because it has constituted a direct and open challenge to dogmatic exclusiveness, wherever found. Through three centuries Friends have been a problem to the creed makers. Here are people who give considerable evidence that they are Christians, but they break the neatly stated rules. How can you define Christians as baptized persons when some whose Christianity is everywhere recognized have never been baptized, at least not in the sense intended? *Thus experience, produced by experiment, checks dogma. This truly is scientific method.*

There is in the world today a great deal of fruitless argument, especially between Protestants and Roman Catholics, over the question what the true church is and who is in it. The Quaker experiment cuts straight across this argument by the application of the experimental test. Do you want to know whether a group is part of the true church? Very well, note whether they love each other; note whether their hearts are quickened by the love of the Living God; note whether they show that they have the mind of Christ in them. No other credentials are needed. If these are lacking, all reference to historical origin and development is meaningless anyway. Ask, of any group, not how it got here, but where it is now. The golden text of all this emphasis on radical veracity is found in a memorable sentence from the pen of Robert Barclay who, like Fox, was impatient of artificiality.

> "It is the life of Christianity taking place in the heart that makes a Christian; and so it is a number of such being alive, joined together in the life of Christianity, that makes a Church of Christ; and it is all those that are thus alive and quickened, considered together, that make the Catholic Church of Christ."[1]

Such a sentence suggests nothing to be added or taken away. Anyone can use this test now, for it belongs to all. It is one of the best fruits of the experiment.

At first the experiment had no name and needed none. Fox simply declared what his own experience showed to be true and a few listened. The beginning of ordered preaching, confined to the English Midlands, occurred in 1647. Fox was only twenty-three, but it was a great year in his life. It was just three hundred years ago that this serious young man, disappointed at what the recognized clergy were able to give him, realized, with the suddenness of revelation, that, since he was a child of the Living God, he was not dependent on what these men could or could not do. He saw that there were other sources of the knowledge of God than those provided by a conventional education and that such knowledge was, indeed, open to every seeking spirit. Because the passage which describes this opening is crucial to the radical experiment, and because we are standing now at the tercentenary of this experience, the familiar passage from the *Journal* should be quoted in full:

> "Now after I had received that opening from the Lord that to be bred at Oxford or Cambridge was not sufficient to fit a man to be a minister of Christ, I regarded the priests less, and looked more after the Dissenting people. Among them I saw there was some tenderness; and many of them came afterwards to be convinced, for they had some openings. But as I had forsaken the priests, so I left the separate preachers also, and those

---

[1]Apology, *X*, 10.

called the most experienced people; for I saw there was none among them all that could speak to my condition. And when all my hopes in them and in all men were gone, so that I had nothing outwardly to help me, nor could I tell what to do; then, oh! then I heard a voice which said, 'There is one, even Christ Jesus, that can speak to thy condition'; and when I heard it, my heart did leap for joy. Then the Lord did let me see why there was none upon the earth that could speak to my condition, namely, that I might give Him all the glory; for all are concluded under sin, and shut up in unbelief, as I had been, that Jesus Christ might have the preeminence, who enlightens and gives grace and faith and power...and this I knew experimentally."

In the year 1648 the experiment got its first name, Children of the Light. The small community was so called because Fox was directing his hearers to the living experience of Christ as the Light available for all. This was in no sense a denial of the importance of the Christ of history, but rather an identification of the Light with the Christ of history. William Penn noted later that Friends preferred to speak, not of the "light within," but of the "light of Christ within." It has been well said that "the crux of Fox's discovery was that in the present spiritual reality he was aware of the same living Christ to whom the scriptures and the doctrines bore witness. It was a mystical apprehension of the fact that the person of Christ belongs not only to history at a given time and place, but also to an eternal world into which Fox and his friends knew that Christ had brought them."[2]

This emphasis on the Light, which gave the experiment its first name, was a sound beginning, though alone it was not enough. It is always a sound beginning, because it starts with experience, and all knowledge rests ultimately on experience of some kind. That direct, immediate experience of God, as objectively real, is possible, and that such experience is not a delusion, has been verified by countless men and women throughout the three hundred years of the experiment's duration. The chief means of verification has been the evidence of changed lives. William Charles Braithwaite once wrote that the chief enrichment of Christianity so far made by the Quaker movement consisted in the production and training of a type of character which "goes through life trying to decide every

[2]*The Nature of the Church*, p. 19.

question as it arises, not by passion or prejudice, nor mainly by the conclusions of human reason, but chiefly by reference to the Light of God that shines in the prepared soul."[3] Here is another contribution to the Church Universal which a restricted but radical experiment can make. All Christians now have more reason to trust both corporate and group guidance as a result of the experimental approach.

The second name attached to the experiment, quickly supplanting the first and continuing to this day is the name of *Quaker*. This name, first used in 1650, was clearly given in derision. We have two somewhat different accounts of the origin of the name, though the two accounts are not irreconcilable. According to the *Journal* of Fox, the name was first given by Justice Bennet at Derby, where he was imprisoned for twelve months in 1650-1651, originally on a charge of blasphemy. "Justice Bennett," wrote Fox, "was the first that called us Quakers, because we did bid them tremble at the word of the Lord. This was in the year 1650."

The other account is that of Robert Barclay, who says the name was given because of the trembling which Friends sometimes experienced in their meetings.[4] Apparently the nickname of the Derby judge stuck because it matched an already recognized situation. What was most striking to outside observers was that these people took their faith so seriously that they were shaken to the very center of their lives. The most important thing to be said about their religion was that it *shook* them. They accepted the gospel, not as dull information and not with mere intellectual assent, but as a message marked by terrific *urgency*.

The third name attached to the experiment is equally revealing. If the first name stressed immediate experience and the second name indicated the mood of urgency, the third name was a testimony to the fact of a genuine fellowship. The name which the experimenters came to love most and which they officially adopted was *Friends*. They were, they said, Friends in Truth and Friends of one another; they were therefore the Religious Society of Friends.

---

[3] *Spiritual Guidance,* p. 82.
[4] *Apology, XI,* 8.

That this emphasis on fellowship has been crucial to the entire experiment is easy to see. The inner illumination alone might produce the self-centered and the bizarre, with no outside checks on either ideas or conduct. The sense of urgency alone might produce unbalanced fanaticism. But men and women who submit to the disciplines of fellowship, recognizing the authority of group experience, are largely saved from these extravagances. The lesson of the Quaker experiment is that, while individual mysticism may be dangerous, group mysticism tends to be wholly beneficent. They mistake the meaning of the experiment greatly who suppose it has been primarily a glorification of individual religion, necessary as that may sometimes be. Few phrases were as common to early Friends as the words "one another" and "together." They found that a serious attempt to practice radical Christianity makes men and women temper their own wishes by the wishes of their fellow members. The great mystery, they discovered, is the mystery by which we become "members one of another," not merely in meetings for worship, but also in meetings for discipline. It is very important to note that the fellowship realized in the experiment under scrutiny has not been the fellowship of *individuals,* but the fellowship of *families.* It is therefore radically different from the Shaker movement, which was partly inspired by our experiment, but has now practically come to an end in essential failure. The Shaker movement had no place for families, but the Quaker Movement has always glorified the family. In the days of persecution the children carried on the meetings while the parents were in prison. The Fellowship, then, has kept close to common life with its heavy responsibilities and its opportunities. The fellowship has never been that of the monastery or that of the spiritually elite, but that of common families including men, women, and children devoted to common pursuits.

Though these are the chief names by which the experiment has been known, the names as actually given in history do not exhaust the list of primary features of the movement. One remains to be mentioned, and may best be understood by reference to the word *concern.* Good as the fellowship is, the fellowship would have been a failure if the enterprise had ended there. Friends soon saw that the final justification of the fellowship was the creative way in which it led people into the service of their fellow men. A concern arises when the deep experience of the knowledge of God as revealed by Christ, and especially that knowledge which emerges in the minds of a genuine fellowship, leads those thus shaken to perform deeds of mercy to their neighbors wherever found. Thus the concern accomplishes the marriage of the inner and the outer; it joins, in miraculous fashion, the roots and the fruits of religion. Above all else the experiment has demonstrated that equal attention to both the roots and the fruits is possible and that spiritual health is found wherever this situation obtains.

Where only the roots are emphasized, we have a situation in which people luxuriate in their own religious emotions, developing their inner experiences for their own sake. It is easy for religion to stop here, but when it does, we have little more than spiritual sensuality. It is fundamentally self-centered. Where, on the other hand, only the fruits are emphasized, we have mere creaturely activity, the kind of worldly philanthropy which eventually is little more than professional social service. Friends, in their long history, have often made both of these mistakes, but the major tradition has been the avoidance of both by keeping the connection close. Worship of God is one thing and service of mankind is another, but the first is dishonest unless it eventuates in the latter and the latter is superficial unless it springs from the former. A realization of this has led many Friends to think of John Woolman as our best exemplar. In his experience, more truly than in that of most, great sensitivity to social wrongs stemmed directly from a sense of God's presence and sovereignty. The world is helped whenever any man or any group of men demonstrates the power which this close connection makes possible.

As we analyze the radical three-hundred-year-old experiment in this fashion we come to see it as something in which the separate features are united in one sequence of ideas and events. The order in which the main characteristics of the movement appear is both logical and chronological. There are five steps in the sequence and these constitute the five most important contributions of the movement to the rest of mankind. These can be denoted by the use of five words.

1. *Veracity* is the first word. The lone, struggling George Fox was indeed seeking what William James called "A Religion of Veracity." He could not be content with shams; he saw through the artificial. This drove him beyond the conventional aspects of Christianity. He was impatient of all unreality. This was not the end of the matter, but it was a grand beginning.

2. *Immediacy* is the second word, following directly from the first. Far too much religion is a matter of what people take at second hand from others, without a sense of first-hand knowledge. Radical Christianity necessarily makes men dissatisfied with that knowledge which is "knowledge about" and leads them to seek that knowledge which is "acquaintance with."

3. *Urgency* is the third word in the series. Those who have had a direct sense of the divine presence cannot stand idly by while other men and women go on in relative darkness. Those who seek to experiment with radical Christianity are bound to be shaken out of all easy respectability, shaken to the middle of their lives. It is inevitable that they, in commitment to the will of the Living God, became evangelical in mood and missionary in intention.

4. *Fellowship* is required in such an experiment, especially as an antidote against unprofitable excess. The experiment, to be worthy of attention, must be deeply social. The veracity, the immediacy and the urgency, are all disciplined by the reality of group experience. The radical Christian always recognizes that his fellow members have a stake in his own undertakings and that the normal religious unit is the group.

5. *Concern* brings the entire series to a climax. Even with the fellowship, the movement would fail apart from a strong sense of service to needy men and women. So long as the fellowship is the fellowship of the concerned, it is saved from becoming self-congratulatory and self-regarding. This is the completion of the experiment. It *is* the *Religion of Veracity,* it *is* the *Children of the Light,* it *is* Quakers, it is the *Society of Friends,* but still, more truly and more comprehensively, it is *The Fellowship of the Concerned.*

III

Here, then, is one experiment which, by its own inner logic, has shown what the essential elements of a living witness are. As developed in history these elements are five, and they are five which can be applied to any serious undertaking anywhere. They are not the unique possession of one particular movement. We may go farther and express the serious doubt that any redemptive movement can be efficacious *unless* it involves these five elements no matter how much more it might involve. Thus we are helped, by one historical experiment, in the creative dreaming demanded by the needs of the modern world. Whatever a redemptive movement may be called, wherever it may be produced and whatever its external form, it cannot be truly effective unless it includes *Veracity, Immediacy, Urgency, Fellowship,* and *Concern.*

The actual Quaker Movement has often been a poor thing. It has advanced and receded many times in three hundred years of tumultuous history. Seldom have all five of the vital elements been equally incorporated in the Movement. Frequently Friends, who began by cutting the ecclesiastical red tape, have been unhappily successful in producing their own variety. Friends have failed on several occasions to maintain the sacredness of their own fellowship. Sometimes they have forgotten what it is to be *Quaker,* persons utterly shaken in their lives, and have settled back with a complacent sense of superior virtue or attainment. But in spite of all these failings, many of which continue to this day, the movement has, from the beginning, carried within it a singular promise. The deep inspiration has always been the ideal experiment, by which current failures have been judged, and this ideal experiment is that which requires the five names for its adequate depiction. The Fellowship of the Concerned has not been fully realized in the historic Society of Friends, but there has always been this haunting vision, inherent in our Quaker life.

Sometimes Friends have allowed themselves to become a mere sect, with little interest in other Christians, but this was not our first position nor is it our last. Quakerism, when true to its own genius, has been ecumenical in spirit, concerned with the entire human family and mindful of the words of our Lord when He said, "Other sheep have I which are not of this fold." It is worthwhile to remember that the experience of George Fox on Pendle Hill, in 1652, was interpreted by William Penn in a wholly ecumenical manner. Penn said that Fox "had a vision of the great work of God in the earth, and of the way that he was to go forth to begin it." This is precisely the vision which each one of us craves for himself. Fox, as Penn interpreted him, was not thinking merely of those who might be called Quakers, but of all men everywhere, made in God's image even though they know it not.

"He saw people as thick as motes in the sun, that should in time be brought home to the Lord; that there might be but one shepherd and one sheepfold in all the earth."

This is the ecumenical ideal; this is the Christian ideal. At this juncture of history it seems far from realization, but it is eternally valid. This is the clear vision which makes us know how imperfect our present condition is. Perhaps it is the vision without which a people will perish.

What we seek, then, is the emergence of the true church, the company of loving souls, exhibiting the mind of Christ. Our fondest hope is that our own modest experiment of a few centuries may facilitate the emergence of this sacred fellowship. We do not seek to make all men Quakers. Quakerism, as we have known it, is not good enough. What we desire is that all men be brought into a far more ideal society than any we have known. If Quakerism ever helps to usher in that larger and more ideal society, it will have done its peculiar work. What we seek is not, therefore, merely our own perpetuation, but that Fellowship of one Shepherd and one sheepfold. But, since that Fellowship is still in the making, our modest testimony continues to be needed. The best thing we can do for the modern world is to demonstrate to all that a Fellowship of the Concerned is actually a live possibility. Our function, in the Church Universal, is to help keep alive the faith in this possibility.

Chapter 3

The Vocation of Barclay

Leslie Stephen, in his valuable article on Robert Barclay, in the *Dictionary of National Biography,* refers to the *Apology* as "the standard exposition of the principles of his sect," but this is a compliment which Barclay would have felt bound to reject. When he decided upon his life work he did, indeed, dedicate himself to the exposition and promulgation of principles, but he never thought of these as the principles of a *sect.* Instead he was devoted, he thought, to the presentation of objective and universal truth.

> "That which, above all things, I propose to myself is to declare and defend the *Truth;* for the service whereof I have given up and devoted myself, and all that is mine; therefore there is nothing, which for its sake (by the help and assistance of God) I may not attempt."

His books were, he supposed, an exposition, not of some peculiar thing called Quakerism, but rather of radical Christianity, shorn of its superstition and artificiality.

We wholly mistake the Quaker movement if we think of it as modest in its hopes or even in its claims. It is impossible to find a prominent early Friend who supposed that Friends were starting one more "denomination" of Christians, one sect among others. Instead they one and all believed that they were the humble instruments by means of which God was leading the Christian world, as a whole, out of its apostasy and into the light. Their purpose was not to add to the number of individual

---

The substance of this address was presented as the Tercentenary Barclay Lecture of London Yearly Meeting, held at Edinburgh, in August of 1948.

Quakers so much as to arouse the conscience of Christendom, producing a new and *true* Reformation which should go much farther than the Reformation inaugurated by Luther and Calvin.

Many of the early Friends undoubtedly believed that this great new Reformation, which might turn both Catholics and Protestants to a new life, which was also the old life of primitive Christianity, was actually in process and that a new day was dawning before their eyes. There is abundant evidence that the persecuted Quakers, especially those gathered in the prisons, lived in an atmosphere of high expectation and enthusiasm, as though the kingdom were "at hand." Thus Colonel Barclay, writing to his son from the Aberdeen Prison early in 1676 said,

> "We are all in health & refreshed daily by the Lord's power-fully appearing in & amongst us & in a wonderful & unexpected way visiting us by his overcoming love to the gladning of our hearts & making us willing not only to believe but to suffer for his name's sake."[1]

In the same month, Robert Barclay wrote to David van den Emden, a Dutch scholar, as follows:

> "I doubt not but there are many in these parts & thyself amongst others that are abundantly satisfied & convinced that the Protestant Churches needs a reformation in the main not much less than the Roman did at what time Luther appeared, seeing the same life of ungodliness & Spirit of Anti-christ pre-vails generally over them, in being purely delivered from which consists a real & sound reformation."[2]

What he wanted was a *genuine* Reformation. It would come not by the *brain* and not by *opinions*. It seemed to be very exciting. What if there could be a revolution, not *in* ideas, but *beyond* ideas? What if there could be a revolution such that it would be *permanent*?

George Fox went about saying that the Lord, Himself, had visited His people. Though he believed in the possibility of continuous and therefore immediate revelation, as against the notion of a closed canon, he was convinced that in his troubled time, the living Christ had appeared in men's hearts in an

---

[1]*Reliquiae Barclaiana,* VIII.
[2]Ibid, p. 25.

unusually vivid way. It was an apocalyptic time, not in the sense of any intimation of the imminent end of history, but in the sense that God was using the crisis to make His will known in a peculiar way. The responsibility of those who experienced such revelations was not to themselves alone, and not to their little sect, but to the entire race of mankind. How vividly Barclay shared the notion that he was living in a time as favoured as it was confused is shown by the following sentence from the *Apology*: "Therefore the Lord God, who, as he seeth meet, doth communicate and make known to man, the more full evident and perfect knowledge of his everlasting Truth, hath been pleased to reserve the more full discovery of this glorious and Evangelical dispensation to this our age."[1]

Barclay was at pains to point out that this glorious contemporary divine visitation was not dependent upon the character or talents of the individual men, called Quakers, who seemed to be its instruments. On the contrary, they were, like the Apostles, humble and unworthy men. God had, it seemed, chosen even illiterate men and mechanics for this purpose, in order that "no man might have whereof to boast" and that all might see clearly that the work was truly God's work. Perhaps the finest and most succinct of Barclay's statements about the way in which he and his fellows came to know the "Truth" is that in which he says that "the knowledge thereof hath been manifested to us, by the revelation of Jesus Christ *in* us, fortified by our own sensible experience, and sealed by the testimony of the Spirit *in* our hearts."[2] 2031503

From such a central conviction missionary activity arose as a natural consequence. Here was a conception of life suitable to all and meant for all; therefore men everywhere must be reached. It was no accident that the early Quaker missionaries spread out in all directions and that every member was, in some sense, an evangelist. They were living at a great time and they were entrusted with a great work. It was no accident that colonies were established in the new world; it was no accident that they went directly to labourer, Pope and King. There seemed to be a great turning in the direction Friends desired,

---

[1] *Apology,* V, VI, 10.
[2] Ibid.

though sometimes enthusiasm ran beyond the sober fact. The actual results of the frontal attack on Holland were neither marked nor permanent but George Fox, in reporting it wrote, "There was a mighty concourse, and the Mystery of Iniquity and Godliness were opened and declared in the Demonstration."

All Quakers of the period shared this flaming purpose, but it was left to Robert Barclay to state it more brilliantly, especially during the months of his long winter imprisonment at Aberdeen when he had time to brood on his great subject. At this time, March 17, 1677, he wrote to Emden, hoping to convince him of the truth of the message. The exciting fact, he said, was that *men's hearts could actually become the place where God dwells.* How thrilling if this were really true and if men could somehow comprehend the glory of it! To Emden he wrote:

> "We have found a great care laid upon us from the Lord that we be not preachers or fomenters of meer opinion but that our testimony may reach to and raise up that of God in the heart to the bringing it up over the bondage & thraldom of sin there, that so the life of righteousness may be propagated & increased in the earth that the Lord may receive the hearts of the children of men for a clean habitation to himself."[1]

People, thought Barclay, who are the recipients of a great revelation and the bearers of a message needed by all men, cannot confine their energies to sectarian interests. He did indeed, encourage some organization of Friends, as Fox had done earlier, but this was not primarily for the sake of Friends. The organization was not an end in itself, but simply a rational instrument, designed to increase the effectiveness of those who went about their main business, which was the conversion of Christendom. The only excuse for the Society of Friends was the improvement of the missionary task. The efforts of most Friends, according to this doctrine, were necessarily directed, not to their fellow Friends, but to the people of the world, high and low, wherever they could be found and reached. Barclay meant most of his readers to be *non-Quakers,* and he by no means confined his speaking to Friends' meetings. His friend and associate, Andrew Jaffray, spoke of Barclay as having

---

[1]*Reliquiae Barclaiana*, p. 26

"some weighty services at several steeple houses."[1]

Writing in Aberdeen prison, with the prospect of the great attack on the European continent planned for the following summer, Barclay mused on the problem of sectarianism and came to some conclusions. "A sect," he said, "is a company of people following the opinions and inventions of a particular man or men, to which they adhere more, and for which they are more zealous, than for the simple, plain and necessary doctrine of Christ." In short, it is the essence of a sect that it is non-universal, whereas those who preach radical or universal Christianity, neither Roman, Genevan, nor Anglican and "hold forth principles and doctrines consistent and agreeable thereunto, are and may truly be esteemed mere Christians, and no sect."[2]

By this standard it seemed clear to Barclay that those whom the world chose to call Quakers were no sect at all, but plain representatives of essential Christianity. What the world called Quakerism was nothing queer or novel, but primitive Christianity revived, as Penn was to term it. Those for whom Barclay spoke were emphatically *not* "Foxites." They did not arise, in a movement, because of the eloquence of one man or from their own human decision, but rather "from their mutual sense of this power working in and upon their souls." The passage in which Barclay describes the spontaneous use of the new fellowship which is a foretaste of ultimate Christian unity, is one of the noblest of his prison writings:

"Now these people, who hold forth the principles and doctrines hereafter to be mentioned were not gathered together by an unity of opinion, or by a tedious and particular disquisition of notions and opinions, requiring an assent to them, and binding themselves by leagues and covenants thereto; but the manner of their gathering was by a secret want, which many truly tender and serious souls in divers and sundry sects found in themselves; which put each sect upon the search of something beyond all opinion, which might satisfy their weary souls, even the revelation of God's righteous judgment in their heart to burn up the unrighteous root and fruit thereof. . . . And so many came to be joined and united together in heart and spirit in this one life of righteousness, who had long been wandering in the several sects;

---

[1]*Truth Triumphant*, Testimonies.
[2]*Universal Love*, Section V.

37

and by the inward unity came to be gathered in one body: from whence by degrees they came to find themselves agreed in the plain and simple doctrines of Christ."[1]

In this remarkable passage it is especially important to note the order of development. It is Barclay's claim that neither doctrine nor organization was primary, but that both of these followed as consequences from the supreme fact which was the moving and shaking inner experience. The movement came not by deliberate intention and not by human ingenuity, but by the natural cohesion of those whose hearts were in living converse with the Spirit of the Living God.

As it is a serious mistake to suppose that Friends, in the beginning, looked upon themselves as one denomination among others, so it is also a mistake to suppose that they considered themselves Protestants or a part of Protestantism. Because of his peculiar training, Robert Barclay had a larger part than most in clarifying this particular point. By education he was as well acquainted with Catholic as with Protestant doctrine, and it is essential to an understanding of his career to realize that he reacted *equally* against *both*. He considered it his vocation to carry on a running fight against both sides in the Reformation dispute *and to lead Christian men into a new day in which both Catholicism and Protestantism would be superseded.*

Barclay was careful to point out explicitly the evils and mistakes of both sides of the current controversy. His criticism of Roman Catholicism is direct and severe. The main evils of Rome are (1) the arrogance of exclusive claims, (2) the self-glorification which expects obeisance and lives in ostentatious grandeur and (3) the persecution of non-conformists. The net result is that they are far from the spirit of Christ, for there can be no Apostolic succession without Apostolic reality. "It is abundantly manifest," says Barclay, "that there can be nothing more contrary to this universal love and charity, than Romish principles, and that no man of that religion, without deserting his principles, can pretend to it."[2] Indeed Roman Christianity is really a sect because of its lack

---

[1]*Universal Love*, Section V.
[2]*Universal Love*, IV, 1.

of universality or catholicity, this lack being demonstrated by its persecution of those outside it.

Barclay finds that Protestantism is equally far from essential Christianity. Though the parts of Protestantism differ widely in some respects, all follow the same practice, like that of Rome, of persecuting dissenters "not permitting one another the free exercise of their conscience in their respective dominions." In Great Britain, he says, this fighting is the more amazing in view of the fact that nearly all are united on doctrine, being "in a sense all Calvinists." Not having doctrines to fight over the British Protestants fight over the matters of church government and of ceremonies.

A second Protestant evil is that "not only common both to Lutherans and Calvinists, but even to those sub-divided Calvinists (I mean the Episcopalians and Presbyterians)...to wit, the pressing after and seeking to establish a national church." The result is that "a man cannot be a member of the state without being a member of the church also; and he is robbed of the privileges, which he ought to enjoy as a man." The result is that ecclesiastical irregularity is punishable in the same way that a heinous crime is punishable.

Barclay's third objection to Protestantism, and the one he felt most deeply arose from the fact that Protestantism, as he knew it, was based on the proposition that God has limited to a few of mankind the necessary means of salvation. The doctrine of limited election, the precise opposite of universal love, was the object of Barclay's bitterest attacks throughout his life. This Calvinist doctrine seemed to him so monstrous as to be actually blasphemy. We find frequent references to this not only in his published books, but also in his correspondence. It was his chief point of attack in trying to get a harvest of seekers in Holland and Germany. In November, 1677, after the expedition in which he had been joined by Fox, Keith and Penn, John Durie of Cassel wrote to Barclay specifically on this sore point as follows:

"The point of difference between me and the ministers of this place is the moderation of my Judgment that I cannot close with them in the rigid Doctrine of one absolute Reprobation of the greatest part of mankind from all eternity to be damned only for this end that God will shew his wrath they hold that all who are

39

not elected & called to the knowledge of Christ by the Gospel as
we are are without all mercy predamned."[1]

Barclay admitted that there were varieties among
Protestants in the degree to which the doctrine of Reprobation
was held, but the central question is whether God ever
withholds from any men the power and grace to be saved, so
that their failure is a *necessary* failure. To believe so would be
to believe that God could deny His own nature as revealed by
Christ.

> "Now I say, whoever are of this mind (as all Calvinists general-
> ly are) cannot justly pretend to universal love; for seeing they
> limit the love of God to a small number, making all the rest only
> objects of his wrath and indignation, they must by consequence
> so limit their own love also: for God being the fountain and
> author of love, no man can extend true Christian love beyond
> his."[2]

Thus Barclay saw about him two kinds of apostasy. The
Christian world was bitterly divided and both sides were alien
to the spirit of Christ. The basic Roman heresy was the
exclusiveness of its claims and the basic Calvinist heresy was
the limitation on divine love.

> "For these two principles, to wit, that of there being no salva-
> tion without the church among papists, and this of absolute
> reprobation among protestants, are the very root and spring,
> from whence flows that bloody and anti-christian tenet of perse-
> cution for the case of conscience; and therefore both it and they
> are directly contrary and diametrically opposite to the true,
> Catholic, Christian love of God."

This last phrase may be taken as a clue to Barclay's entire
position. He proposed to go beyond and behind both
Catholicism and Protestantism to the "true, Catholic,
Christian love of God." This is all he sought and this he
believed men generally might be called to. The very defects of
the existing and competing faiths showed the way back to
essential Christianity. A true, catholic Christian would never
make exclusive claims for his own human organization, he
would seek simplicity rather than the intentional
impressiveness of ostentatious grandeur, he would never
arrogate to himself the honour which belongs alone to Christ,

---

[1] *Reliquiae Barclaiana*, p. 37.
[2] *Universal Love*, IV, 3.

he would never engage in persecution of others for religious differences, since the spirit must be free, and he would never believe or act as though the Eternal God could will the destruction of any of His children made in His image. Those who follow such principles waiting patiently and reverently for the immediate touch of God's life upon their own, are in no sense sectarians, but simple followers of Christ.

Barclay's particular vocation arose from the fact that he felt able, by virtue of his training and experience, to reach the learned world with this thrilling and revolutionary conception of what the Christian life might be. How seriously he planned the use of his powers in waging a literary campaign is shown by the fact that he shared his ambitions with George Fox in correspondence. Fox wrote to him about his strategy of distributing the books once they were written and the older man's letter reveals a high sense of expectancy. Barclay seemed as one sent to the kingdom for this purpose. We must not suppose that the *Apology* and the *Theses* of which it is an amplification were addressed to *Quakers*. On the contrary they were aimed at influential people, the *magnum opus* being prefaced by a letter to the King, which is a direct effort to convert *him*. The *Theses* were addressed, not to laymen, but to the theologians of the day. "To the Clergy of what sort soever, into whose hands these may come; but more particularly to the Doctors, Professors, and Students of Divinity in the Universities and Schools of *Great Britain*, whether *Prelatical*, *Presbyterian*, or any other: Robert Barclay, a Servant of the Lord God, and one of those (who in derision are called *Quakers*) wisheth unfeigned Repentance unto the acknowledgement of the Truth."

It is clear that Barclay was, in this enterprise, aiming at a high goal. He employed the dialectic of trying to show his adversaries that they really adopted his conclusions without admitting them. If he could win the assent of the leading theologians they might guide their flocks with them away from the pseudo-Christianity which was so common and unto the "simple naked truth" of genuine Christianity. It was because of this basic strategy that Barclay wrote his most important book in Latin; his enterprise was neither modest nor local. When Dr. Nicholas Arnold, Professor of Divinity in

Holland, replied to Barclay's fifteen Theses, Barclay issued a rejoinder in Latin at Rotterdam in 1675. This explains also his many trips to the European continent; essential Christianity was bound, by its very nature, to transcend the limits of Anglo-Saxon culture. This, too, explains his interest in influential people like Princess Elizabeth. It looked for a while as though she would come over to the simple truth and bring many others, particularly the Labadists, with her.

The fact that Barclay wrote so much in Latin and often with a rather severe logical form does not mean that Barclay was parading his knowledge. We misunderstand him wholly if we think of him as interested in what we now call pure scholarship. Penn, if it was indeed he who wrote the Preface to *Truth Triumphant,* felt constrained to defend Barclay against the charge of parading scholarship, explaining his manner of writing wholly on strategic grounds. "The method and style of the book," the Preface says, "may be somewhat singular, and like a scholar; for we make that sort of learning no part of our divine science. But that was not to show himself; but out of his tenderness to scholars, and as far as the simplicity and purity of the truth would permit, in condescension to their education and way of treating those points herein handled; observing the apostle's example of becoming all unto all." Sewel, the Dutch historian, supports this conclusion as follows:

> "And though his natural abilities were great enough to have made him surpass others in human learning, and so to have become famous among men, yet he so little valued that knowledge, that he in no wise endeavoured to be distinguished on that account. But his chief aim was to advance in real godliness, as the conversation I had with him hath undoubtedly assured me: for I was well acquainted with him."[1]

Barclay's vocation was not to present and defend the Quaker point of view, but to marshal evidence on a few great points in such a way that it would be convincing to all with open minds. He was not concerned with the structure of the "Quaker Church," a term he did not use, but rather with the structure of *any true church,* anywhere in the world. He was concerned with what ought to be and with what the experience of a few

---

[1]William Sewel, *The History of the Rise Increase and Progress of the Quakers,* 3rd Ed., Vol. II, p. 234.

demonstrated *could* be. In the *Apology* the word "Quaker" appears but seldom after the title page. Barclay would have been surprised to hear that he had described something called "Quakerism." What he supposed he was presenting was merely straightforward Christianity or *God's Truth*. This could, he thought, be stated in such a way as to appeal to any person, regardless of national background or sectarian bias. He believed that the truth lay in a mediating position between Evangelicalism and Rationalism, between Authority and Freedom, between Mysticism and a Bible-centered faith.

The vocation of Barclay was important, not only in his own life, but in the developing Society of Friends. It was his appeal to the learned world and not some treatise for sectarian consumption that came to be looked upon as the best exposition of what Quakers believed. This had the effect of saving Quakerism from many abuses and uncritical assumptions. Because he was writing for the thoughtful people of the world, many of whom were savagely critical, Barclay had to be extremely judicious in his statements. This led to balanced judgments as against fanatical *cliches*. This factor, more than most others, served to keep Quakerism within the main stream of Christian history and Christian thought, and helped to resist the temptation to become a form of esoteric mysticism, with a neglect of historical Christianity. Eventually Quakerism *did* become a sect, in spite of Barclay's efforts to the contrary, but because of his central thought, Friends have ever since been restive under the sectarian status and the basis of a new conception has been provided for later generations.

Chapter 4

The Conversion of Quakerism

In one sense the Friends' World Conference begins this week, but in another sense it has been going on for five years. In one sense it is a gathering of nine hundred people, but, in another, it includes thousands who have worked and studied and prayed for this hour. The conviction that a Conference ought to be held arose out of a remarkable experience in 1947. The Friends World Committee for Consultation, when it met at Earlham College in September of that year as the first representative gathering of Friends after the end of the war, began like any other gathering, but it did not end so. In the midst of the week attenders found themselves bogged down by the perplexing decisions and with a heavy agenda still before them. Instead of plodding along, it suddenly seemed right to forget the business for one or two sessions and to engage instead in what became an unusually deep time of worship. The problems were speedily handled in the remaining sessions and the conviction became unanimous that we ought, in spite of all the signs of danger on the political horizon, to begin to look forward to a world gathering of Friends in a few years time.

Now the intermediate years have come and gone, and, stormy as they have been, the faith of 1947 has been justified. We understood all along that our time is destined to be one of continuous strain, but we believed that Christians, who claim to be rooted and grounded in the conviction that nothing can separate us from the love of Christ, ought to plan confidently

This message was the opening address at the Friends' World Conference, held at Oxford, England, in 1952.

rather than to submit to fears. We cannot alter the strain, but we can live confidently *in* and through it.

As we have faced these days at Oxford we have been quite unashamed in our expectancy. If any cynic thinks that we have expected too much, we are content to bear his scorn, for we believe that ours is a world in which the living God is seeking to bring us, both individually and collectively, into a new life and we are guilty of inadequate faith if we rest content with anything less. *If we merely have another good meeting, with pleasant fellowship and some good speaking, and no more, our gathering will have been a failure.* If we have just another conference, with routine business and sensible decisions, we shall be hindering rather than accomplishing the divine purpose as it has become clear to us with increasing vividness in these tumultuous years. Both men and movements *can* be reborn, and such, we firmly believe, is God's will for us.

We have begun, this summer, the fourth century of the Quaker Movement and, we earnestly desire, by God's help, to begin it aright. Since it will not be sufficient to copy anything which has been known during the three centuries which are gone, wholly new and surprising developments may be in store. One of the most heartening features of the Christian religion is its capacity for reformation and renewal *from the inside.* The salt almost loses its savour, but never loses it wholly. When the body of Christ seems almost lifeless, new powers suddenly emerge and vitality reappears. Since this phenomenon has occurred too often in Christian history to be accidental we may, accordingly, expect it again, though it is not for us to know the time or the place of its appearing.

What we pray for, as we enter the fourth century of our undertaking, is not primarily a new insight or a new doctrine. We have excellent insights and we have doctrines that have stood the test of critical examination. We do not need a new message: what we do need is new life.

Because it is exactly three hundred years since the time of the great awakening in the north, to which we owe so much, we have re-examined that surprising development of 1652, and we realise that the doctrine then taught was not new nor did its promulgators claim that it was. What they did was to take an old doctrine and *believe* it with such thoroughness that their *lives* became new. We have emphasized, and rightly so, the vision of the young Fox as he stood, apparently alone, on Pendle Hill, but we have not emphasized sufficiently the possibly more important experience as he joined others in the tavern at the foot of the hill. There at last he began his most effective ministry to others and he began it with an electrifying announcement. The announcement was to the effect that "Christ was come to teach people himself." The consequent excitement came primarily from a change in *tense.* All Christians were already agreed that Christ *had come,* and many dreamed of a time when He *would come* again in the future, but Fox was aware that the most exciting tense is always the *present.*

The idea that Christ can lead and teach His disciples *now,* and not merely in the past or in the future, ought not to be a surprising idea, since Christ Himself declared, "Lo, I am with you *always,*" but the idea seems always to be overwhelming when genuinely grasped. It would be overwhelming to *us,* if we should grasp it at Oxford in 1952. Every Christian generation which has felt the present, day by day leadership of the living Christ has become explosive and irresistible, however great the surrounding apathy or resistance. To this experience the Bible testifies abundantly. Witness the experience recorded at the end of the fifth chapter of Acts, which does so much to explain the victory of the gospel in the ancient pagan world. There we learn that some of the Christians, after being set free by the wise interference of Gamaliel, and having been beaten, were told to remain silent, but, like all who know the leadership of Christ in the present tense, they could not obey such an injunction. The climax of the story, in Doctor Moffat's striking translation, is this: "And not for a single day did they cease to teach and preach Jesus the Christ in the temple and at home."

It was this kind of intensity that the gospel had both predicted and verified. The prediction was made by John the Baptist and it was verified by the first Christians as they met directly with their risen Lord. The Gospel according to St. Luke mentions this experience of *enkindling* near the beginning and again near the end. Near the beginning the Baptist says, "I indeed baptize you with water but *he* shall baptize you with the Holy Ghost and with fire." Near the end

47

the disciples say to one another, "Did not our hearts burn within us, while he talked with us by the way?" Baptism is enkindling: the mark of the baptized person is the burning heart: the mark of infidelity is coldness and complacency.

The Friends in the summer of 1652, actually believing that Christ had come again to be their teacher, evidently lived day by day in a triumphant and infectious mood similar to that described in the Book of Acts. They rode on the top of a mighty wave. Our present meetings, of whatever type, are a poor substitute for what was going on at Swarthmore three centuries ago. They sang, they laughed, they suffered gladly, they loved mightily. Howgill's great words, when we hear them now, succeed both in thrilling us and in making us ashamed.

> "The Kingdom of Heaven did gather us, and catch us all, as in a net and His heavenly power at one time drew many hundreds to land, that we came to know a place to stand in and what to wait in, and the Lord appeared daily to us, to our astonishment, amazement, and great admiration, in so much that we often said one to another, with great joy of heart, What? Is the Kingdom of God come to be with men? And will He take up His tabernacle among the sons of men, as He did of old?"

It is possible to stress too greatly the life and words of the first generation of Friends, if, by so doing, we are merely glorifying the past, but this is by no means necessary. The wholesome procedure is to understand some of the conditions of that amazing vitality, in the hope that the miracle may be repeated in our own day in ways suitable to our situation. The only excuse for remembering yesterday is our hope for tomorrow.

In the eyes of the world Quakers are a mild harmless people, but how shocked many would be to read the works of that young man Edward Burrough, whom his contemporaries called "a son of thunder and consolation." This man, who died in prison before he was thirty, gives us a glimpse of something very like a spiritual *storm*.

> "And while waiting upon the Lord in silence, as often we did for many hours together, with our hearts and minds towards Him, being stayed in the Light of Christ within us, from all thoughts, fleshly motions, and desires, in our diligent waiting and fear of His name, and hearkening to his Word, we received often the

pouring down of the spirit upon us, and the gift of God's holy internal spirit, as in the days of old, and our hearts were made glad, and our tongues loosed, and our mouths opened, and we spake with new tongues, as the Lord gave us utterance. . . ."

Today some Friends engage in silent worship and some Friends sing, but three hundred years ago the sons of thunder and consolation did *both*. The same vivid sense of Christ in the present tense which made them speechless also made them shout. Our shame today lies in the degree to which both our silence and our singing are conventional religious gestures, rather than spontaneous responses to the tremendous fact of a present Christ.

The double mark of the renewal of Primitive Christianity, initiated by Fox, was the *spiritual high tension on the one hand and the continual outreach, on the other*. Perhaps these are always the marks of validity when Christian vitality reappears. The inner intensity would have been mere spiritual self-indulgence, if Friends had hugged their experience to themselves, but this they could not do. They preached in churches, they preached at fairs, they preached in prison. Swarthmore was indeed their base, and their place of renewal of strength, but it was primarily a place to go *from* rather than a place in which to *remain* in comfort. Friends of Burrough's hard-hitting day had no notion of becoming a sect or of developing into a highly respected denomination, with well managed institutions and pious anniversaries. They sincerely believed that their function was to unite all Christendom by the recovery of Christ in the present tense. The vision was gloriously ecumenical. Friends were personally humble, but the responsibility was *great*.

In no seventeenth century writing is this anti-sectarian emphasis more clear than in Penn's brilliant preface to the Journal of George Fox. Fox's own account of the Pendle Hill experience is disappointingly brief, and Penn seems to have undertaken deliberately to provide a fuller account, based, no doubt, on what Fox had reported to him personally of the experience. It is difficult to believe that Penn would have been so specific under any other circumstances. Fox, himself, tells how, on a hilltop, he had a specific leading to specific *places*, but Penn indicates that, prior to this, there was a general sense of a world wide mission for the recovery of Primitive Christianity. "In 1652" Penn says of Fox "he had a vision of the great work of God in the earth, and of the way that he was to go forth to begin it. He saw people as thick as motes in the sun, that should in time be brought home to the Lord, that there might be but one shepherd and one sheepfold in all the earth." In accordance with this conception, every Friend was a missionary and a preacher, in so far as the vision was appreciated. The Valiant Sixty were only striking examples of a general rule. Friends of three hundred years ago existed, not primarily for the sake of a little separate society, but to reach the world by every valid method available.

Judged by this standard, contemporary Quakerism is guilty of treason to a great dream. Thousands of modern Friends not only do not think of themselves as missionaries, but are a bit uncomfortable when that word is mentioned. Does it not sound a little pompous, they ask, as though we had a superior message to give? After all, they say, since other people have a right to their own opinions, we ought not to proselytize. We make a virtue out of our dullness and boast discreetly of our policy of spiritual aloofness. Thousands of those who call themselves Quakers not only never *quake* themselves, but never shake anyone else. The very idea seems somehow undignified or lacking in respectable reserve. We might be a bit ashamed of Edward Burrough if he were here today.

Now this we must say as clearly as possible: the modern tendency to avoid evangelization or to feel condescension towards those who engage in it is a *heresy*. It is a sign, not of Christian humility, but rather of cowardice, of snobbishness and of spiritual decay. Never forget that Jesus, after he had told the little redemptive society on the mountain-side that they were the salt that could keep the world from decay, gave as His first command the following: "Let your light so shine." We know a great deal about the religious mentality of our generation when we realize that this word of our Lord is highly unpalatable to many. Frankly, it almost seems to be in bad taste! But nevertheless it is the Lord's word and, if we are restive under it, we should examine ourselves to see where the trouble lies.

Our generation supposedly avoids over-pushing, but what

this masks is really fear of dedication. It is part of the cleverness of sin that it so easily wears the mask of virtue. If the mask is not torn off in any other way it may be torn off by the winds of doctrine in the current world storm. We may be sure that the characteristic young men and women on the other side of the iron curtain are not backward in being evangelists for their dangerous and inadequate, but strongly gripping cause. Listen to a letter from China, written by a young Chinese man, twenty-one years old, formerly a Christian convert. Here is the letter:

"Now I am no longer the former man you knew. Apart from my body, which is the same, my whole mind and thought have changed. I have become a new man in the Classless Revolution Pioneer Corps, a loyal believer of Marx-Leninism. I shall never live for myself alone, but for the masses. What satisfies my aspirations now is the progress of a happy socialism to a communist state. In this new teaching I have found unimaginable blessing and happiness. I very much hope that you will examine this question.

"I am very sorry but I must inform you that I no longer believe in God nor worship Him. I can no longer address you as a religious brother, but I send you my revolutionary love."

If we were really to experience the double baptism of the spirit and of fire, we should be equally enkindled, but for a better gospel. We should speak in clubs, in colleges, in churches, in labour groups: we should write; we should outthink as well as outlive the pagan world. Not for a single day would we cease to preach and to teach Jesus the Christ *in the temple and at home.*

Thousands of Friends ought often to be away from their meetings, doing the very work in the world for which the meeting exists. If we burn ourselves out in this enterprise, what does it matter? Better men and women than ourselves have done so. Perhaps that is part of what the baptism by fire means.

If such a policy of universal missionary activity among Friends both young and old should become the standard expectation, tremendous results might be achieved in a very short time. It is not conceivable that the only people in the world who will respond to the emphasis on the present leadership of Christ, for which the word Quakerism is a mere label, are those now enrolled in the Society of Friends. There must be millions in various denominations whose convictions are the same as ours are supposed to be, many of them far more loyal to the vision than we are. There must be other millions who are seekers, in the important sense that they have become dissatisfied with a pagan or secular order of civilization, but have not learned of a type of Christian experience which is a simple dependence on Christ, without the artificialities of professional claims, and which expresses itself as a radical democracy of the spirit. If people are searching for this, and if we believe it is possible, we are unfaithful servants when we fail to publish the saving truth.

It is heartening to know the degree to which the convictions which unite us here are acceptable to large sections of the general public today. Often they are more acceptable without the Quaker label than with it, but it is the content rather than the label which counts. One of the most evident signs of Christian vitality during the past year has been the spontaneous appearance, in widely separated areas, of important conferences on the ministry of the laity, an idea in which our contribution is generally recognized. Thousands will accept gladly today the exciting idea of the ministry of all Christians, if only we are willing to present this New Testament conception in language understandable to modern man. The same is true in regard to the Christian equality of men and women in the common ministry, to the Light of Christ in all, and much more. The opportunities for such messages are so numerous that Friends are now forced to decline the majority of invitations. This is a great shame. We ought to have hundreds of men and women, prepared in both mind and heart to take the opportunities when they come. Sometimes a few *are* prepared. How wonderful that Elizabeth Vining was prepared and ready when the opportunity came for some Christian to be tutor to the Crown Prince of Japan! How heartening that Clarence Pickett and others were prepared and willing when the opportunity arose to perform conciliatory service in consultation with the Assembly of the United Nations! Here are two examples of a method ideally suited to our complex modern life. The method is that of penetration at every point where penetration is possible. Some must train to become penetrators in academic life of the great pagan universities of our day, some must learn to work inside the labour movement, many must enter government service. And each one who is really committed to the power and wonder of Basic Christianity will use his work in the world as a means of personal ministry, whatever his means of earning a livelihood may be.

It is our Christian conviction that we do not need to wait for some special season of God's leading, because we believe that the guiding hand of God is *always* reaching out to us. The only reason for failure is *our* failure to meet the conditions. As we have analysed the period of enkindling which we are especially remembering this summer, we have found two primary conditions, the inner intensity and the continual outreach. It is surely God's will that we seek deliberately and prayerfully to meet these conditions and then the event is in the hands of God. This gives us our double emphasis. On the one hand we must cultivate the intense life of love in our Christian homes and in our particular meetings. If there are no homes there is no nation and if there are no local fellowships there is no Church of Christ. On the other hand we must make these homes and meetings places of *reaching*. Today we must do honour to Marmaduke Stephenson who died on far away Boston Common, but we must do equal honour to his devoted wife in Yorkshire who maintained the base from which he went and to which he would have returned so gladly. *The base is fruitless without the outreach: the outreach is fruitless without the base.* It is in equal emphasis on both that recognition of Christ's present leadership is most likely to be known.

The Quaker movement must change, and it must change because today it is not good enough! We must change as individuals and we must change as a religious society. Though for some members this will involve a radical alteration in mode of life or even physical location, such outward change will not and ought not to mark the ministry of all members. Many ought to stay where they are, engaged in the same secular work and devoted to the building up of their own homes and families, but with a new intensity. The struggle of our time goes on at every point, including those points with which we are most familiar and not merely at those which are glamorous

53

or so far away. But whether we travel or whether we stay at home, there must be a change in the sense that the spiritual pressure is vastly increased, the conviction of vocation deepened, the ministry of common life glorified. We may go on doing the common tasks, but we shall do them as men and women continually engaged in the Christian ministry. Thus we can emerge from the comfortable security and try to reach the men and women near and far, who are sceptical, the men and women who are antagonistic, the men and women who are indifferent. These, to use Penn's phrase, are "thick as motes in the sun." The building up of the local meetings is very important because we need centres of power and invigoration, but our meetings become idols if they are destinations when they ought to be starting places.

It is because of thinking of this kind, based on the manifest need of a radical change, that the general subject of this World Conference is "The Vocation of Friends in the Modern World." Whatever uniqueness this conference already has lies almost wholly in the recovery of the idea of 'Vocation.' If the conference in these ten days really accepts this idea, it will be truly unique. Meeting in this university town two years ago, those of us who were on this Conference Committee came early to the unanimous decision that Vocation was the Christian word for our time. We are sure that we have a vocation and we seek reverently, though persistently, to know what it is. Knowing it we pray for the power to answer it.

Vocation, more than any other word in the vocabulary of religion, bridges chasms which have divided Christians into adherents of half-truths. In the first place it transcends the division between those who, according to one contemporary theological fashion, stress only God's initiative, and those who, according to another, stress only man's responsibility. When we feel the significance of the old Latin word, "Voco-vocare" we understand a situation in which we know that we cannot plan merely in our own power, but must indeed wait for God to call us, yet we understand, equally, that we are responsible because God, in His love, has made us so that we can resist His call or be deaf to it, as the case may be. In so far as we emphasize vocation, neither side of the divine-human encounter is minimised or forgotten. Thus we may be enabled to avoid the special dangers of both neo-orthodoxy and of humanism.

The second way in which the idea of vocation transcends differences regards the relative importance of the inner and the outer aspects of religion. There have always been those who have so stressed the inner experience that they have, in effect, neglected the work of service in the world, and there have always been those, on the other hand, who, impatient with the life of devotion, have hurried on to feed the hungry or to clothe the naked. Now the point about the idea of vocation is that it unites, in an indissoluble bond, the inner and outer aspects of our faith. The experience is inner and spiritual, because it is God who *calls,* but the experience cannot be genuine unless it eventuates in *work.* Call is a verb which has about it a fundamental transitivity: the person who is called is always called *to* something: he has a calling and his calling is some form of service to his fellow men, who are likewise being called to membership in the body of Christ. In so far as Friends have developed a theology, it has been one which gives equal emphasis to God's grace and to man's responsibility and which stresses equally the roots and the fruits of religion, holding both in one context, in a manner so vividly demonstrated in the life of John Woolman. The word vocation is shorthand for this theology.

Let us be done, forever, with the notion that the Society of Friends is a satisfied little body, highly self-regarding, and secretly proud that it is small. Could we, at Oxford, make our witness that we believe in the veracity and the adequacy of the central message which, by a process of history, has been placed in our charge? We want it to prevail! We hope that in a hundred years from now, when Friends assemble to begin the fifth century of their movement, they will be many times as numerous as we are now. We desire this, not in order to glorify a movement and not to augment a human institution, but out of concern for the seeking millions to whose spiritual interests we are disloyal if we keep still when we ought to make our witness felt.

The movement which now starts on a new hundred years must become much stronger or it will soon be far weaker. There is one thing we cannot do, and that is *stand still.* We must have a larger conception of our vocation or we shall eventually become deaf to any call.

There is a vivid parable for our time in the new wonder drugs to which some of us owe the lives of those who are most dear to us. The physicians have learned that some of these, with great potential effectiveness, have no effect whatever when administered in small doses. If we give a little we are wasting even that little and might well give none, because the body of the ill person so soon accommodates itself to the small dose. But if we give a really big dose, the disease germs are overcome.

What we need now is the big dose. The old ways are not good enough. Our ordinary ministry is not that of the sons of thunder. We listen and assent and often do nothing. We shall not be saved by slightly better monthly meeting sessions and by slightly better religious education. The hour is too late and the illness too entrenched. Only the big dose will be worth administering now.

What we need is a baptism. What we require is a sense of vocation so compelling that the Society of Friends becomes a valiant hundred thousand in the midst of the turbulent twentieth century. *That* would indeed be the big dose and that, by God's grace, would suffice.

The ordinary aeroplane *cannot* go slowly. If it tries to go slowly it falls to the ground. If we do not go faster and higher, the time will come when we do not go at all. The words of the late Stephen Vincent Benet are so appropriate to our situation at this hour that they might almost have been written for us:

> "Life is not lost by dying,
> Life is lost, minute by minute, day by dragging day,
> In all the thousand small uncaring ways.
> The loves we had were far too small.
> Something is loosed to change the stricken world,
> And with it we must change." [or else]

56

Chapter 5

Quaker Evangelism Today

Among the great and notable evidences of new religious vitality which have appeared in the middle of our troubled century, a new emphasis on mass evangelism has been one. In the long run it may not turn out to be as revolutionary as the growth of the lay ministry, and it may not be as healing as is the ecumenical movement, but it has already made a conspicuous difference. In any case it has brought religion back into the general news and it has done so in a beneficent way. Millions who seldom think of religion, are well aware of the phenomenal success of the London Crusade and of the great meetings earlier this year in Glasgow. The news has been striking because mass evangelism has had astonishing successes at the very time when it was widely supposed that it had become as obsolete as the fringed-top surrey. There has been a resurrection of something which the majority evidently supposed to be gone forever.

The reappearance of successful mass evangelism provides an appropriate occasion for a serious and careful consideration of the practice of evangelism in the total Christian Cause. What kind of evangelism is *living* and what kind is *dead*? What methods can we honestly approve and what methods are we bound to condemn? Are there new approaches, more fruitful than hitherto employed, which we should be able to make, if only we were sufficiently imaginative and bold? What are the major lines which the evangelism of the future should follow?

This address was delivered as the annual Quaker Lecture at Indiana Yearly Meeting, in August of 1955.

Though these questions ought to be asked, and though answers ought to be attempted by any serious Christian, each must make the reappraisal from the vantage point of his own experience and background. In this particular lecture the starting point is that of Quaker life and history. By Quakerism I mean a peculiarly insistent effort to rediscover and re-enact primitive or basic Christianity. When I refer to Quakerism I do not mean a movement of people marked by a peculiar speech or dress, or even by a peculiar form of worship, but rather a movement marked by a peculiar effort to come into first-hand contact with the Living Christ. Other groups, of course, have made some claim to do this but among Quakers it has been the controlling and central motive. Quakers have been imperfect men and women, often sharing the vices as well as some of the virtues of their neighbors, but the purpose which inspires their efforts has been a peculiarly exciting one — the purpose to be taught by Christ Himself.

This is why we have no hierarchy, for Christ had none. This is why we have no real distinction between clergy and laity; this is why we have no separate holy days, this is why we have simple meeting houses rather than shrines; this is why we have no special group called "religious" which are separated from ordinary life; this is why we hold that the love of one another is the chief test of discipleship. Insofar as we are honest we admit that we fail in all these things, but Quakerism has performed a signal service for all Christendom by reaffirming this standard of Basic Christianity in many generations. It is in the light of this standard that we must re-examine the practice of evangelism in our day. What would be the evangelistic emphasis of Basic Christianity?

Our question is not merely what Quaker evangelism should be, but what any truly Christian evangelism ought to be. The question of how Friends should be evangelistic would not be a very important question, for that is a merely sectarian question. What we ask is how any person who seeks to make the Cause of Christ prevail should undertake the task. Do we approve the holding of carefully planned gatherings covering a period of several days or even weeks, with the avowed purpose of producing new converts to the Christian Cause? Do we approve the encouragement of public witness to decision in the use of the mourner's bench? What is our conviction about the necessity of follow-up activities? Is it possible that visitation evangelism is more effective, in the long run, than is mass evangelism? Or can both be encouraged together? To what extent should the ordinary meeting for worship be evangelistic in mood and intent?

In facing all these subsidiary questions we can start from a common agreement regarding our basic premise, the conviction that an unevangelistic Christianity is a contradiction in terms. It is reasonable for sincere Christians to question or even oppose some *methods,* because some of them are indefensible, but it is not reasonable for any sincere Christian to oppose the spread of the gospel. A wholly static religion is already dead. It is essential to the human situation that, while we may move forward, and while we may move backward, there is one thing we cannot do: we cannot stand still. A faith that has ceased to advance is already in retreat.

Any Christianity in which the members are a self-satisfied little group, unconcerned about reaching others with a vital and transforming message, is a heretical group. Whatever they may have, they do not have the mind of Christ. By their complacency they demonstrate that they do not really care for other persons and they demonstrate equally that their own faith is not one which shakes them. In short, however much they value a famous name, they are not *Quakers.* A Quaker is one who is so shaken in his own life that he is forced to try to shake others, bringing to other lives the inner excitement which has meant so much to him. Because we seek to share what we really prize, it follows that the alleged Christian who is not engaged in the sharing, has nothing which he really prizes. All that he has is a conventional Christianity and this is something which is not worth the effort required to keep it going. If I cannot be an infectious Christian I'd rather give it up entirely. The middle ground is unattractive because it involves all of the inhibitions without any of the fun.

As we reconsider the practice of evangelism in the light of what we know of basic Christianity we realize that there is much that can be said, but there are three points of especial

59

significance. These constitute the essence of the present lecture.

The first point is that of freedom, especially freedom from convention. When you think of evangelism, do not think of one special form. We must try to go behind the form to the crucial experience. If we have the spirit of Christian freedom we shall not be limited to any one approach.

One particular evangelistic form may be accurately described as follows: A series of meetings is announced, with a persuasive speaker as the chief evangelist. In these meetings it is hoped that there will be a cumulative effect, leading to public decisions for the Christian life on the part of several. Arousing songs are used, a favorable atmosphere is developed and, at the close of each address, an appeal is made to "come forward." Those willing to make this public witness then approach the platform where they are encouraged to stand or kneel in prayer and are joined there by more mature Christians who seek to help them to achieve a mood of full surrender. Frequently a spirit of exaltation is exhibited by the entire group. The result is usually called a "revival."

Many western and middle-western Quakers have had numerous experiences of this kind, because it was introduced among us in the time of our grandparents, largely under Wesleyan influence. Something of the spirit of the camp meeting soon appeared whenever Quakers came together in large numbers on the frontier. This has often been looked upon as the introduction of an alien spirit into Quakerism, but it was actually far closer to the great meetings of the seventeenth century in the north of England than it was to the tame gatherings which developed later. Much of the fire of Wesley had appeared in Fox a century earlier.

Most of us are well aware of the strengths and the weaknesses of the conventional revival. It is sometimes the occasion of sharp differences among us, because some look back on such practices with gratitude for the beginning of true Christian experience, whereas others look back with horror. Those who look with horror usually do so because they remember occasions when they were conscious of what seemed to them unethical psychological pressure. Some are revolted by the showmanship which they have observed or by their suspicion that the evangelist was more interested in conducting a successful revival, for the sake of his own prestige, than in the real welfare of those whom he sought to influence.

If we approach this matter in the mood of freedom from convention we come up with an answer somewhat as follows. The conventional revival of the last two or three generations has done much good and it has done some harm. Both its upholders and its critics are right. Either a blanket endorsement or a blanket denunciation would be foolish and wrong. Because there are people who would be quite outside the Christian movement today apart from some such effort, we are thankful for what was to them a means of grace. At the same time we must admit that some exhibitions of mass evangelism have been flagrantly dishonest. When all eyes except those of the evangelist are closed, it is easy for him to "see" hands raised that are in fact not raised. No doubt some would defend this as a means to a good end, but it seems very far from the spirit of Christ. The desire to overcome reluctance by giving the impression of a swelling tide of decision may be understandable, but the Christian ethic cannot permit such a neat division between dishonest means and noble ends. It would be better to have no "decisions" than to stoop to shady tricks.

Wisdom consists in seeing that the revival, though valuable to many when honestly conducted, is only one means of Christian evangelism. Bondage consists in limitation to one way, when actually there are many valid ways. Some who react violently against mass evangelism may find new life as the result of steady attendance at a small prayer group, such as those which meet weekly in the Quiet Room of the Earlham Meetinghouse. Some who are allergic to emotional songs can be deeply touched by the obvious affection of ten or a dozen people meeting with a minimum of showmanship.

Others, perhaps a majority, find that the new life, when it comes, arises from reading particular books or from walking and talking and praying with particular individuals. This was the original Christian pattern when Andrew "first found his brother Simon." Of all of the forms of evangelism, personal evangelism is the best because it tends to be most enduring.

The effect of a really dedicated life concerned with mine is hard for me to forget.

It has been said that we may, in the future, refer to this present year as "the year when Mott died." The death of this marvelous man, so used by God to reach others and particularly those of student age, makes us think again of the way in which he was reached. The person who led John R. Mott into a full Christian commitment, so that he would later influence thousands, was a British cricketer, who visited Cornell in Mott's undergraduate days. It is doubtful if the cricketer had any idea what God accomplished through his faithful witness.

It is unfortunate that a good many of our young people think they are opposed to evangelism when the truth is that they are opposed to one particular kind. It is helpful to realize that what seems to us a standard procedure may be fairly new in history and by no means intrinsic to the entire Christian enterprise. The revivalistic pattern, described earlier, is of relatively later origin and has not been exhibited at all in most parts of the total Christian community. Certainly it was not practiced in the time of Christ, and we cannot imagine Him in the role of a professional revivalist. He did speak sometimes to great crowds, but not many were added to His movement in that way. After His earthly life was over, and the Christians gathered, the company numbered only about a hundred and twenty. Not many of the five thousand remained. Most of those who were enlisted were apparently reached one at a time.

What we must be set free from is the notion that evangelism is a special enterprise. It must, instead, be a constant, never-ending effort on the part of all Christians. Special efforts no doubt help, human nature being what it is, but the purpose of sharing the conviction and consequent new life ought never to be relinquished. As you enter an ordinary weekly gathering of Christians it would be good for each to pray that it might be an occasion for the impartation of new life to someone, perhaps himself.

Whenever we as Quakers tend to be puffed up by the generous things our neighbors tend to say about us, part of *The Seven Storey Mountain* ought to be required reading. The part to which I refer is that in which the author, Thomas

Merton, tells of attending a Friends Meeting when he was an urgent seeker. Later, as you know, he became a Roman Catholic and now resides in the Trappist Monastery near Louisville, Kentucky. Little did Friends know that day that they were being given a chance by a sensitive and eager soul. Little did they know that they were tried and found wanting.

Merton's account of the Quaker Meeting he attended makes us squirm or blush each time we read it. The meeting was dull, lifeless, conventional. There was no appeal to Christian discipleship, no humble prayer; there was a secular description of a tourist visit to the Lion of Lucerne! If I thought, as Thomas Merton evidently thought, that his experience of Quakerism was characteristic, I should be as willing to give it up as he was.

Would Merton's experience have been different if he had come into *your* gathering? Or would he have found dull lifeless faces there too? I often wonder if others of Merton's kind have attended my meeting, but were too kind to report what they heard and saw.

What we need is the freedom to be evangelistic at all times to be emancipated from received forms, and to reconsider what Christian evangelism would be if we could start again from the beginning, with no preconceived notions of what it ought to be.

The second important point to make is that the evangelistic gospel must be the total gospel. Much supposed evangelism has been inadequate because it has appealed to only one phase of Christian experience. Sometimes the evangelist says, "Come to Christ," but does not show in detail what coming to Him involves. At the worst, then, it is a mere incantation. Sometimes the appeal is merely emotional and fails accordingly, for though Christianity does involve the emotions, as marriage does, it involves much more. The mistake of conventional evangelism is not that it requires too much, but that it requires too little.

The new life we are seeking, with God's help, to produce in ourselves and others has both an inner and outer aspect, and we must encourage both of these at once. The inner aspect concerns the life of prayer, of solitary meditation and of personal commitment. This is what the great classics of Christian devotion are about. All of the saints have understood

63

that the new life must begin within. Deeds of service often become mere philanthropy when they are not religiously inspired; external religious acts become meaningless when they no longer proceed from the heart. Thoughts are more important than deeds because thoughts produce deeds.

But a Christianity limited to inner devotion would be a sickly plant. The outer deeds of service are necessary to give authenticity to the devotion. What we desire, then, is a total life in which the roots and the fruits are perfectly united and neither is stressed without the other. Mere prayer without action is self-indulgent; mere action without prayer is superficial. The good news we seek to share is the news that the total combination is possible. When we appeal to men to enlist in Christ's cause we appeal in the light of this combination.

It is a great shame that we have ever allowed ourselves to contrast the individual and the social gospel. We need, on the one hand to be personally converted, but, on the other hand, we need to demonstrate the gospel in our labor relations, in our politics and in our business. The separation of these two ought to be shocking. This is one of the reasons why Alan Paton's novels of South Africa move us so deeply. *In Too Late the Phalarope,* the father of the hero has a great deal of individual religion. He prays; he reads the Bible daily; he is regular in attendance at public worship, but his religion seems to have no relevance to his relationship to his rebellious son or to the black people who work for him.

In this same vein we must make sure that our total evangelistic appeal includes the head as well as the heart. Honest religion includes honest thinking. One of the best ways to conduct a special evangelistic enterprise is to organize a preaching mission in which the intellectual appeal of the gospel is presented. Some will never be reached in any other way. T.S. Eliot, whose conversion was a great event in contemporary cultural history, has told us that in his case he became a Christian first of all because Christianity answered more questions than did its various alternatives, and that the emotional overtones came later.

This would not be standard experience in all cases, but we can at least be sure that it is necessary to meet the needs of the sincere doubter. No matter how emotionally satisfying

Christianity is, I am sure that I should give it up if I ever became convinced, as Sigmund Freud was, that it represents a pleasing illusion. I'd rather espouse the harsh truth than the rosy illusion of wishful thinking. There must be many others who are like me in this regard. In any case the evangelism we seek must be such as can appeal to the whole man. The only gospel worth spreading is the total gospel.

The third point to make about evangelism is that it must be undertaken with passion. Some things in this world can be done with calm detachment, but they are seldom the best things. In the past we have made much use of "light" and "seed" as figures, but the figure of the inner fire is better than either, so far as the spread of Christ's kingdom is concerned.

One fire kindles another and sometimes the burning is almost irresistible. The best evangelistic device in all the world is a deeply devoted person who enkindles others because he has himself been kindled. William Penn expressed this in highly quotable form by saying of the early Friends, "They became changed men themselves before they went out to change others."

Sometimes, in the modern world, we have been ashamed of passionate attachment, supposing the position of cold objectivity to be more intellectual, but in this we are wrong, because much is revealed to the loving heart that is hidden from the wise and prudent. In the deepest matters you do not understand until, in the words of President Eisenhower, "your energies are pledged." Little is accomplished in Christian outreach until men and women feel such a concern for other people and for the growth of Christ's kingdom that they are truly on fire. There is something to be said for being quiet; there is nothing to be said for being unmoved and unconcerned.

When we try, as we often do, to discover the secret of the amazing vitality of men like Fox and Barclay three hundred years ago, we are helped by noting how far they were from cold detachment and how unapologetic they were about Christian passion. This is well exhibted by the following words of Robert Barclay, which appear in his private note-book, which I have been fortunate enough to find, and which are now published for the first time:

"Many and deep are the considerations which have been and are upon my heart concerning you. Great and inutterable is the travail of my soul for you that it might be well with you and that your eyes might be opened to see and behold the disposition of this day of the Lord, that your ears might be unstopped to hear the language thereof, that out of the spirit of this world and the worship that proceeds therefrom, ye may be gathered unto the Lord to be guided and led by His spirit, which is the new covenant dispensation for which end am I drawn forth in love to put some things before you."

The language of the young-laird of Ury seems quaint, but there is no misunderstanding his meaning. We might not put it just the same way, certainly we should not write such long sentences, but the truth is that we have not begun to understand what evangelism is if we do not feel as Barclay felt. Beyond all methods is the *conviction and the concern*. If we have these we are inevitably evangelistic in our lives, and if we do not have these, all of our efforts will fail.

Chapter 6

The Paradox of the Quaker Ministry

Observers of the Quaker movement are often surprised and shocked when reference is made to Quaker ministers. Numerous outsiders have supposed that Quakerism is a purely lay religion, somewhat like Mormonism in this regard, or that it is violently anti-clerical. This, of course, only shows that such people have not engaged in any serious study of Quaker history.[1] There were many persons *called* ministers in the first generation of the Society of Friends in the seventeenth century; there were renowned ministers during the long quietistic period, John Woolman and Elias Hicks being prime examples; and there is today the practice of recognizing special gifts in the ministry in the great majority of contemporary Quaker bodies. For about 75 years the larger body of Friends has accepted, as part of its policy, not only the practice of recording the gifts of ministers, but also a system of pastoral leadership. The Quakers who employ pastors are far more numerous than those who do not. The pastoral system has been adopted not only in many parts of the United States,[2] but in mission lands, including those supported by Friends who, at home, reject the pastoral system. Pertinent illustrations are those of Pemba and Japan.

This message was presented as the annual Quaker Lecture at Indiana Yearly Meeting, in August of 1960.

[1]The ministry in the first generation of Friends was extremely powerful and well developed. Full sermons by leading ministers, including George Fox, were recorded and printed.

[2]73% of American Friends have or seek to have pastoral leadership. The system of pastors is used in 66% of American Quaker congregations.

67

The confusion in the public mind about the Quaker ministry is understandable in view of the fact that the Quaker conception of the ministry involves a fundamental paradox. Early Friends, while they recognized an unusually effective ministry of their own, criticized and rejected a clerical system in which the promotion of the gospel appeared to be analogous to a secular profession. Men in this profession were called "hireling priests," not chiefly because they were supported financially, but because they seemed to make the ministry more of a job than a calling. They found the clerical life to be the shortest route to preferment, to social prestige, and to political influence.

One might suppose that Fox and his colleagues would have gone the whole way, in opposition to the professionalized clergy, and to have rejected the idea of the ministry entirely, but this is precisely what they did not do. They elected, instead, to stress, at one and the same time, the dual conception that all men and women, in Christ's cause, are ministers, and that some are ministers in an especial sense. The humblest member was therefore expected to be prepared to follow the divine call, whether in the market place or in the meeting house, but a few were recognized as having unusual responsibilities because they had unusual gifts. It is good, in this connection, to read again the ringing words of William Penn when he said, "It is a living ministry that begets a living people; and by a living ministry at first we were reached and turned to the Truth."

After the return of Fox from America, he set up the "Second Day Morning Meeting" for men ministers, in order for them to supervise books and to distribute the ministry. They believed in divine guidance, but they also believed in using their human powers to do some deliberate planning, in order to make their movement more truly alive. They thus established a kind of pastoral system, with the purpose of nourishing the various flocks. Though no salaries were paid, there were family allowances, even in the earliest period, particularly in connection with long journeys like that of Marmaduke Stephenson to America. The support of his family was one of the major concerns in Stephenson's mind when he felt his surprising call which led, ultimately, to his death by hanging on Boston Common.

From the beginning, then, Friends have accepted the paradox of a ministry which is both specialized and universal, holding that the two conceptions, while different, are not mutually contradictory. Much of the glory as well as the tragedy of the Quaker movement has centered in this paradox. It has been a condition of power, when deeply appreciated, but it has, unfortunately, led to separations when it has not been fully understood or admired. The clear lesson of our history is that, whenever we have relaxed the tension of this paradox by settling for either conception in isolation, *we have declined.* This needs to be spelled out in some detail.

Whenever we have glorified the specialized ministry to the neglect of the universal ministry, we have weakened our position, by failing to develop the powers of the rank and file. A man as great as William Penn did this, without intent. His sense of responsibility was so urgent that, at the Blue Idol meetinghouse, he would sometimes start speaking on entering the building, without even a perfunctory pause in a seated position. Obviously this kind of leadership harms the more modest members by discouraging vocal participation on their part. In an even sadder way, many pastors among Friends today, particularly those who have no feeling for Quaker history, assume that they will be inspired to speak fifty-two times in a year, while the bulk of the members will never be thus inspired. In such ways the universal ministry is discouraged and an important phase of the gospel consequently denied.

The danger, on the other side, is equally great. This is the danger of so stressing the lay aspect of Quakerism that the specialized ministry is not encouraged. In practice this often leads to *no* ministry or to a ministry so fragmentary and so secularized that the meeting for worship begins to have the mood of a political forum. Recently a sensitive woman explained why she refused any longer to attend a particular meeting. It seemed to her to become a mere discussion, with a striking absence of reverence, of praise, and of prayer. Accordingly, she began to attend a little Protestant church in the country, where at least she could hear scripture, sing ancient hymns of Christian witness, and enter into vocal

69

prayer.

The most common result, where there is no strong emphasis on a specialized ministry, is that the messages given tend to be trivial and merely anecdotal. Many of us groan inwardly when, in such a meeting, we hear the familiar opening sentence, "As I looked out of the car window on the way to meeting. . ." This highly personalized approach is often superficial and it is superficial because it does not rest on any serious and sustained effort. It is shoddy because it is fundamentally easy. The branches of Friends who have given up recognizing a ministry are more vulnerable to this than are others.

The danger of a purely lay conception, without the encouragement of persons who have opportunity to study, in order to go deeper, is brilliantly expressed by de Tocqueville when he says:

> "None but minds, singularly free from the ordinary cares of life — minds at once penetrating, subtile, and trained by think-ing — can, even with much time and care, sound the depths of these so necessary truths."[3]

In practice, the pastoral system is, like democracy, the *worst* system, with the exception of all of the others.

I had the great privilege of attending London Yearly Meeting during the historic sessions of 1924, when the practice of recognizing ministers was officially abandoned. The argument presented was that the recognizing of a few would lower the general level of the ministry, because the many would thereby cease to feel responsible. I have visited meetings in Great Britain on six different occasions since that decision was made, and it is my considered conclusion, on the basis of first-hand experience, that the intended improvement did not occur. It is important to know that the life of a religious society can be killed in more than one way. There are scores of local meetings in which, because no individuals feel a strong sense of personal responsibility, there is often nothing of a deeply spiritual nature in the ministry at all. I have often been in meetings wholly devoid of vocal prayer, of reference to Scripture, of Christian teaching.

Of major importance for the health of the entire Quaker movement is a careful consideration of the philosophy of the

---

[3]Alex de Tocqueville, "Democracy in America," Part II, 17.

ministry, but this is something which we have neglected shamefully. The universal ministry is a great idea, one of the major ideas of the New Testament, but the hard truth is that *the universal ministry does not come to flower except when it is nourished deliberately.* We go deeper into the paradox of the Quaker ministry when we recognize the fact that the nourishment of the universal or lay ministry is the *chief reason* for the development of a special or partially separated ministry. We cannot have an effective universal ministry of housewives and farmers and merchants, simply by announcing it. It is necessary to help *produce* it. The only way in which to produce it is to train a minority for this holy task. We need ministerial leaders, not because we reject lay religion, but because we believe in it so powerfully that we propose to do something about making it genuine.

All who have any close connection with Friends in either Philadelphia Yearly Meeting or London Yearly Meeting know of the violent opposition expressed by their members to the pastoral system. Some go so far as to say openly that those who have pastors are simply not Friends at all, and that, they say, is the end of the matter. They do this, sadly, because they see so clearly that Quakerism is not worth the trouble if it is merely another little Protestant sect, with the same kind of ministerial responsibility found in larger groups of Christians. If we are going to be like the Presbyterians and Methodists, why not, some say, join them and be done with the farce of separateness to no purpose? After all, we should then have a better trained ministry, a better planned order of worship, and a far better financial arrangement.

Having heard this argument many times, I am bound to say that, if the assumption is correct that our pastoral system in the main body of Friends is merely a poor reflection of what the stronger Christian bodies intend, the critics are right. But it is the assumption that we need to examine as carefully as possible. Is it a fact that Friends pastors are simply poorly prepared Protestant clergy, accepting a leadership in which the ministry of the regular members is denied or trivialized? Yes, in some areas this is a fact. I can name meetings in both Indiana and Western Yearly Meetings in which the Friends pastor has no notion at all of a unique function and is, in fact, a conventional clergyman. He is a member of the local ministerial association, he allows himself to be called "Reverend," he speaks every Sunday, he leads the prayer meeting, he becomes the official pray-er on ceremonial occasions, he does all the visiting that is done in the congregation, and, worst of all, this does not disturb him in the slightest. He supposes that this is the way it should be. Often he has come from another tradition, and is so ignorant of Quaker history as not to know that for the first two hundred years of Quaker life *there was not one pastor*. Sometimes he does not even realize that he represents something very close to that which George Fox and his early associates denounced.

Having faced this situation honestly, we need to go on and say that the pastoral system, though it may be altered, cannot be and ought not to be abandoned. Apart from it, thousands of living Quakers would not be Quakers at all today. Most of the congregations of the Middle West which refused to inaugurate pastoral leadership ultimately died. This is the hard fact, and we cannot argue with history. It is also important to point out that there is an extremely beneficent kind of leadership of which the violent critics of the pastoral system are often entirely ignorant. In practice the Quaker pastor is, in many instances, a modest man who lives on much less than he could earn by giving his full time to some secular occupation and he is frequently forced, for financial reasons, to engage in part time work in industry. He never feels like a clergyman, accepts no title, and expects no deference. He does not dress in any clerical garb and he is known principally by his first name. He works steadily and unobtrusively to educate the young, to keep the Sunday School as strong as possible, and to encourage the gifts of others. Frequently he teaches an adult class and seeks to raise the level of Christian reading in the homes of the members. He is self-effacing because he feels called to build up the life of the group, knowing that, unless someone does it, consciously, it will not be done at all. He believes that the greatest ministry is that of the dedicated group.

It ought to be recognized, also, that in both London and Philadelphia Yearly Meetings, in which there is such criticism of the pastoral system, there are people in some local congregations who, without definite appointment, are carrying on pastoral work which is similar to that just described. Sometimes there is a man or woman, with sufficient means to have freedom from secular employment, who accepts the call to constant nourishment of the powers, the gifts, and the spiritual depths of others. That Rufus Jones performed such a service at Haverford for many years is known to all who ever attended meeting when he was present. The fact that he earned his living as Professor of Philosophy did not make him any less of a pastoral minister.

Though the division between pastoral and non-pastoral Friends seems too great and often so sorrowful, the truth is that there is far more unity of aim as between the moderates on both sides of the dividing line than there is between the contrasting factions within each group. The extremes are indeed very far apart, but, fortunately, there are many who are not extreme. The more successful meetings of Philadelphia and of Indiana Yearly Meetings have much more in common than either has with its particular fringe group. The fringe group in Philadelphia Yearly Meeting is the secularized society which has nothing but contempt for evangelical faith, while the fringe group in Indiana Yearly Meeting is the Fundamentalist congregation which has drifted so far from basic Quakerism that it does not even know what a silent meeting is.

One way out of our present dangers, difficulties, and divisions lies in the rediscovery and consequent embodiment of a conception of the ministry which is truly unique among religious movements. We do not need to seek a foreign way, but only to understand the way inherent in Basic Quakerism. Always our hope lies in a "third way," a way which avoids the heresies of the right as well as the heresies of the left.

The mistakes we made seventy-five years ago, when we started a system of pastoral leadership was not the mistake of providing better ministerial care. That was obviously needed. The meetings were dying for lack of intelligent concern for the spiritual welfare of the members. My evidence for this is more than hearsay, because of what my mother, who is still living, has told me of the struggle which occurred in the time when she was a girl. I know, from this source, that the first pastors brought immense relief, that they represented to the young people of two generations ago a victory over the dead hand of tradition which was terribly stultifying, and that the coming of pastors ended the exodus of Quaker young persons into other denominations.

Though the reasons for the pastoral system were good, a gigantic mistake was made. The mistake was that a fundamentally alien system was taken over, almost intact, from other Christian bodies. The result of this borrowing was that recognized Quaker ministers began to perform duties almost identical with those of conventional Protestant clergymen. Often they had less professional education and such poor remuneration that they had to support themselves on the side, but the *functions* seemed to be the same. The one striking exception was that the function did not include the celebration of the Eucharist, or the performance of water baptism, but even these were adopted in some parts of northern Ohio and southern Michigan, as they are to this day. It is true that there never was a ceremony of ordination, but "recording" for many seemed to be almost the equivalent of holy orders. The main point was that the Quaker pastor became the responsible head of a congregation, representing it officially on public occasions, conducting weddings and funerals, visiting the sick, and preaching constantly. The natural result was that, in many communities, the rank and file of the members ceased to feel any need of doing these things. They had the immense relief which comes from knowing that some other person is responsible. They, accordingly, could go about their regular business with easy consciences.

What was needed seventy-five years ago was a change, but not the change that was instituted. Now we may be ready for another change, a change as great as that made by our grandparents, yet a change in a very different direction. We shall, whether we live in the East or the West, be ready for a change, provided we face our situation with humility and with honesty. The fact is that, in neither of our conventional systems, have we a right to be proud. We are not really doing well anywhere. We are losing in members, in proportion to national population, and many congregations are static, even when there are hosts of new people in residence. Both the pastoral and the non-pastoral systems are partial failures and the basic paradox is that the degree of failure, in both systems, arises from the same reason. Both, in their conventional form, suppose that the two classifications of layman and clergyman exhaust the possibilities in the Christian society. The only way in which we shall overcome our lamentable division is by a clear recognition that there is a third order. If we had really known this in the nineteenth century the present sad division would not have occurred.

There would seem to be two contributions to Christendom from Quaker experience which are truly unique. The first of these is the meeting for worship *on the basis of holy obedience.* This is not to be found anywhere in the experience of Christians, either Roman Catholics or Protestants, until it was developed in the bold experiment of Friends in the north of England in the middle of the seventeenth century. For people to come together, not to express their own opinions and not to go through a ritual, but to settle down into reverent waiting, out of which comes messages surprising even to the speakers, is one of the most creative experiences which devout men and women can enjoy. It can truly be what Howard Brinton has called "Creative Worship" in which the gathered whole is much more than the sum of its parts, and it may also be what Violet Hodgkin called "The Way of Wonder." The wonder lies not merely in the silence, though this can be healing, and it does not lie in the speaking or praying, though they may be more stimulating than ordinary preaching; it lies primarily in the effort of a group to be truly *obedient together.* This is something so good that we must, if we can, keep it real and thus contribute it to the total Christian community. Some other groups have already adopted this way of worship on some occasions, and for this we are glad. Certainly, this unique experiment must always be kept among all branches of Friends. It is a shameful thing if we go so far into the ways of the world that any who call themselves Friends can be ignorant of this creative way. At the same time we must admit that other ways are good, too.

The other unique contribution of Quakers, and one which we have partially neglected, is a particular conception of the ministry. This is a ministry which has nothing to do with status or honor and in which the entire function is a loving, modest concern for the nourishment of the Divine Seed in each human heart. The good clergymen, in the established churches, undoubtedly perform this noble function, but part of their effectiveness is cancelled by the addition of factors of status, and it was these factors which so incensed George Fox. To this day many clergymen are almost forced into a position of artificiality. They are expected to be the officially religious men, always praying at banquets, always giving the address of welcome and being accorded an ambiguous honor in return. Thousands of lay people refuse to call clergymen simply by their names, without some honorific title. When asked why this is, they reply that to fail to use a title would be lacking in respect. No doubt this is why Christ said His followers were not to use such titles. He saw the danger and warned almost fruitlessly against it.

The true pastoral leader, as Friends in our strongest periods have shown, is not a person of exalted status and certainly not the "head" of the meeting. He is always at work, encouraging this one, teaching that one, walking with another. He may speak on public occasions, but often his leadership is not obvious at all. He will not do anything if he can get another to do it, not because he is lazy, but because the doing will develop the other person, and it is development of others that is always his goal. He will speak if he needs to do so, but he knows that speaking is only one of many tasks which spiritual nourishment requires. He may teach more than he preaches, and he will not be afraid to be silent or to sit within the congregation rather than face it, if he believes this will facilitate the general sense of responsibility. He will have the best education which he can get, but he will not make capital of his degrees or expect that they be used by people who address him. He will resist endlessly being called "Reverend" and will not, in any way, show by dress any distinction between himself and others. He will work very hard, but primarily as a catalytic agent. He will be especially pleased if his work, though effective, is unnoticed.

Here is a noble and difficult ideal. What is important to see is that it is radically different from the ordinary Christian conception of the ministry, yet it *is* a ministry. It is not at all the same as saying that all members have equal responsibility and that mere lay religion is consequently sufficient. The fact is that people cannot have equal responsibility because they do not have equal powers and, what is more important, they do not have equal concern. This unique ideal which is equidistant from "no ministry" on one side and from "status ministry" on the other is really the ideal embedded in the New Testament. The classic statement is that of Ephesians 4:11, 12, where we are told that God has given some men the gift and consequent responsibility of being "pastors and teachers" and that their function is the perfecting of the members for *their* work in the ministry. A pastor, then, in Biblical terms, is a humble person who has a special ability in performing that kind of ministry which helps other people to perform *their* ministry, whatever it may be. When we realize that early Friends were trying very hard to recover the vitality of New Testament Christianity, we are not surprised that they tried to produce a kind of ministry which was equally distinct from both clergy and laity.

One of the finest embodiments of the paradoxical Quaker ideal of the ministry was that of the career of Neave Brayshaw. For many years Neave Brayshaw performed wonders among English Friends, particularly among young men. To share with him in the New Year's Conference at Woodbrooke was a really moving and unforgettable experience. Always Neave was nourishing some tender plant. He would walk with his "laddies" and talk about their faith or their doubts. He did this, not primarily on Sundays, but every day of the year and many who are now leaders of London Yearly Meeting remember this service with gratitude. He was, of course, not called a pastor, but he was doing *pastoral work*. His support, incidentally, came from a Quaker Trust Fund. He represented, almost perfectly, the ideal we are needing so desperately to recover.

The clearest statement of the early Quaker ideal is that provided by Robert Barclay in the *Apology*. After stressing the notion that all Christians must be in the ministry and maintaining that the current distinction between clergy and laity is one which the New Testament does not make, he went on to state that there is needed, in addition to the general ministry, a particular ministry.   Barclay's great words are:

"We do believe and affirm that some are more particularly called to the work of the ministry, and therefore are fitted of the Lord for that purpose; whose work is more constantly and particularly to instruct, exhort, admonish, oversee, and watch over their brethren; and that. . .there is something more incumbent upon them in that respect than upon every common believer."

If Barclay's clear teaching had been followed with any seriousness the crisis in Quakerism, out of which the pastoral system emerged, would never have occurred. The question was not, as some have supposed, whether people with particular responsibility should be paid or not. Barclay received no money, because he needed none, but that did not make his ministry any more spiritual. What is significant is not the means of support, but the fact that some men ought to be liberated from purely economic tasks. Barclay was liberated because he inherited an estate from his father, Colonel David Barclay. The pastor of Knightstown or Wilmington is liberated because the members contribute a house and a modest salary. Uncle Samuel Trueblood, of Blue River, was liberated because he owned a good farm. Obviously these are mere details, and we only confuse the issue when we try to make them central. What is central is loyalty to a holy task, and the task is the spiritual nourishment, without which the redemptive society ceases to be redemptive.

There is reason to believe that we are now ready for a bold new chapter in Quaker history. We have caught a glimpse of a dream of what a true Christian ministry really is, and the dream has begun to possess us. If it does possess us it will make us real Quakers again, because it will shake us to our foundations. We are considering the start of a new kind of educational venture, the first real school of the Quaker ministry in over three hundred years of our history. We have reason to believe that such a school may receive a warm welcome, not only among Friends, but also among many other of our fellow Christians who have been vaguely dissatisfied with the conventional alternatives, but have not fully realized that a potential third order exists. We may receive a particularly warm welcome from those pastors who are deeply disturbed by the role of busy promoter which they now seem practically forced to play, but from which they see no escape.

Because the present conventional system is not really succeeding, people may be willing to give a fair hearing to some genuine alternative.

We are undertaking, not some minor step, but one of great proportions. The new ministry which is one of function rather than status, is not to be the private possession of those called members of the Society of Friends. It must, eventually, belong to all, for it is basic to the total Christian ideal. The ideal was etched by Christ Himself when he girded Himself with a towel and portrayed the ministry of humility. "I have," He said, "given you an example." This is our standard, a standard which we never fully reach, but one which never lets us rest. It is the prime inspiration of the Quaker ministry.

Chapter 7

The Total Gospel

This is not my first opportunity to give the Quaker Lecture at Indiana Yearly Meeting, but it is an opportunity which I prize uniquely. I prize it especially because it comes at the beginning of a new chapter in my life. Twenty years ago I joined this Yearly Meeting, and I have given it all that I could give during these two decades. I especially appreciate the joys and responsibilities of five years in the Presiding Clerk's chair. Now that I am officially retired as Professor of Philosophy at Earlham College, and have been given the title of Professor at Large, I am free to engage full time in what Quakers have always known as the traveling ministry. The ancient term "liberation for service" now has a deeper personal significance for me than it has ever had before. And, as this new chapter begins, I want to say something to my own fellow members which will give you some idea of what I shall try to say elsewhere in different parts of the world. I trust that I may have energy to carry this message across national as well as denominational lines.

The main purpose of this lecture is to try to say something that is both true and important. Only so can we make a difference in the world. There are propositions which are true but trivial, but they are not worth the trouble of our enunciating them. I believe that the Quaker Movement includes, at its heart, truths of great relevance and of great excitement; at least they are exciting to me. I believe, also,

This address was delivered as the annual Quaker Lecture at the 1966 sessions of Indiana Yearly Meeting.

that the Quaker Movement, as we know it now, is only the faint approximation of what it can be. It is a hazy shadow, when it could be a bright light for all Christendom and all the world.

The chief way in which the Quaker conception is exciting is that in which it can be a valid expression of Basic Christianity. Quakerism, when it understands itself aright, is not an odd little sect with a peculiar vocabulary, but a revolutionary effort to represent the Gospel of Christ without distortion. I think Joseph John Gurney, who spoke in this Yearly Meeting with such power in 1837, was wonderfully right when he defined Quakerism as: "The religion of our Lord and Saviour Jesus Christ, without diminution, without addition, and without compromise." As we re-read the words of the Quaker spiritual giants throughout the centuries, we finally come to the striking conclusion that the Gospel of which we are speaking is a total Gospel. What Fox and Barclay and Penn and Woolman and Gurney were expressing was not a compromise between extremes, which would be essentially colorless and tame, but rather a comprehension of many sides of the Gospel because each side is inadequate alone. As I read the story I find that there are four specific ways in which the Quaker vision of wholeness has comprehended, and therefore included, elements which seem, on the surface, to be in conflict, but which in fact are complementary.

1. *The first way in which the gospel must be total is in the union of its roots and its fruits.* There is always a great temptation to stress either the inner side or the outer side of Christianity, to the exclusion of the other. Thus there are a good many people who try to set up some kind of dichotomy between what they call the social gospel and the personal gospel. It is precisely the refusal to accept this dichotomy which has marked the greatness of the Quaker saints, and especially of John Woolman. Woolman's voice was the first clear voice in the English colonies of America to say that followers of Christ must be concerned with the social and economic lives of men and women. He saw the evils not only of slavery, but also of luxury. Some day I hope we can publish a separate volume of Woolman's essays on the social application of Christianity which are wonderfully relevant to our

generation, though not nearly so widely known as is his *Journal*. It is a really amazing thing that this unostentatious New Jersey businessman had the imagination to write his original essay "On the Keeping of Negroes" in 1746, i.e. about 117 years before the Emancipation Proclamation. Woolman wrote his "Plea for the Poor" 200 years before the start of our anti-poverty program. But, at the same time, Woolman's religion involved a deep inner experience of the love of Christ. The Living Christ was a reality for Woolman. He tried not to proceed in the ministry merely upon his own judgment, but to listen to what the Living Christ was saying to him. In his final illness in York he wrote:

> I have been more and more instructed as to the necessity of depending, not upon a concern of what I felt in America to come on a visit to England, but upon the fresh instruction of Christ, the prince of peace, from day to day.

Always, Woolman was as deeply concerned with listening to the inner voice as he was with ministering to the needs of suffering mankind. "Oh! how deep is Divine wisdom! Christ puts forth his ministers and goeth before them; and Oh! how great is the danger of departing from the pure feeling of that which leadeth safely!"

What the Quaker witness has to say to the world is that there is no necessary conflict between worship and work, between the personal and the social, between the inner roots and the outer fruits of a living Christian faith. We see, daily, illustrations of the evils which follow when this totality is rejected. There are, for example, workers in the program of social reform who, when they become separated from the love of Christ, are consequently bitter and vindictive. On the other hand, we see people who are so satisfied with their own inner experiences that they do not see the necessity of the social application of what they have learned in the inner citadel. Quakerism says to the whole world that the parts are evil when separated, but creative when held together. What we must have is a union of the temporal and the eternal. It is easy to see how there is a temptation for these to be separated. Thus, it is possible for a person to say that his only concern is for his eternal salvation. I have heard people say that, because they want to get to heaven, they don't care about anything else. On the other hand, I have known many who claim to have no concern for eternal life, but are eager to do their duty here and now, with nothing but contempt for the kind of evangelism which stresses eternal salvation. What I want to say is that I see no justification for conflict and I believe that many people in the world are looking for a religion which unites the temporal and the eternal in one miraculous whole.

2. *The second way in which the gospel must be total is in the combination of the evangelical and the rational.* Sometimes, in the history of Quakerism, these two emphases have been separated, and the result has always been disastrous. The merely evangelical emphasis, without tough mindedness, leads to superstition and reaction, while the merely intellectual becomes spiritually sterile. It is wonderful to see how the two strands can be combined perfectly in the character of such a person as Robert Barclay. Barclay was entirely evangelical, in the sense that his life was Christ-centered, but he was also one of the most tough-minded of rationalists.

I believe in a religion which is not afraid of personal piety, which is warm-hearted, and even passionate, while, at the same time, it faces every problem which the enemies of Christ can throw in our path and uses all potential rational faculties to face these. For 35 years I have accepted unconditionally the famous dictum of Samuel Taylor Coleridge, who said: "He, who begins by loving Christianity better than Truth, will proceed by loving his own Sect or Church better than Christianity, and end in loving himself better than all."

Though Robert Barclay is perhaps our most distinguished representative of this aspect of totality, so far as 17th century Quakerism is concerned, it is important to realize that we have had an equally striking illustration of such totality in the 20th century. One of the greatest Christian intellectuals of Quaker history was Professor Rendel Harris, famous Biblical scholar, discoverer of manuscripts, first professor of Semitic languages at Johns Hopkins University, later at the University of Cambridge and finally at Woodbrooke. I met him and talked with him in 1939, not many months before he was killed by a bomb in the Battle of Britain. He was an old man, and I knew of his tremendous scholarship and the toughness of his mind. But the thing that most attracted me was the combination of style in which this toughness of mind was combined with a tenderness and an affection like that of a really good child. We understand him better through the following incident: At one time he was walking with his beloved niece and the girl asked him about heaven and the nature of the life everlasting. He said, "My dear, you need not ask about the way to heaven. It will be a conducted tour." Here was a man who, in his own living room, would fall upon his knees in prayer. Tender, loving, reverent, he was also as tough and as hard as could be, when dealing with a text in some difficult language.

Many of us are grateful to the scholars who have given us the successful New Testament translation called *The New English Bible*. One of the most brilliant of their translations bears exactly upon our present point. It is as follows: "Therefore, my brothers, I implore you by God's mercy to offer your very selves to him: a living sacrifice, dedicated and fit for his acceptance, the worship offered by mind and heart." (Romans 12:1). Mind and heart are dangerous in separation, but glorious in combination.

3. *The third way in which the gospel must be total is in its combination of the conservative and the contemporary.* On several different occasions in Quaker history the necessity of this union has been forgotten or neglected, with damaging results. This, for example, was what was happening one hundred years ago in the famous separation between the conservative and progressive Friends. The sad result was that the help which each group needed from the other was suddenly removed and each suffered accordingly. As we try to find our true way, we soon realize that our golden text is in the words of our Lord in Matthew 13:52, when He said, "Therefore, every scribe who has been trained for the kingdom of heaven is like a householder who brings out of his treasure what is new and what is old."

Every sensible person is a conservative! By this I mean that every sensible person wants to retain the gains of the long past rather than to waste them wantonly. It is perfectly clear that wisdom has not been invented in our generation and that the rejection of the old, merely because it is old, is essentially stupid. Everyone who appreciates the Bible understands this perfectly. If there is a contrast between our present judgment and the judgment of the earliest Christians it is conceivable that we are right, but it is not likely. It would require only a little humility for us to recognize the advantage of that which has been tested, and consequently verified, by generations of ancestors.

On the other hand, every sensible person seeks to be contemporary! There is no point in our trying to say anything if we cannot be understood. Thus, we must put new wine in new wine skins. We must understand modern technology, modern science, and modern social movements if we are to be adequate representatives of Christ in our generation.

As we study the Quaker story, we soon see that this combination of conservatism and contemporaneity has marked the finest periods. The earliest Quakers were conservative, just as they were clearly evangelical. They, too, sought to revive primitive Christianity in all of its richness, but they were also contemporary in that they held that the Living Christ had to be encountered in the immediate present. What our experience indicates is that the old is best, even though dressed in new garments, and that the new is undependable unless it humbly learns from the past. The notion that Basic Christianity must be rejected because it arose in another generation is so ridiculous that we could not believe that it would be seriously affirmed unless we saw it in print, as we have seen in the writings of a number of supposed Christian leaders in our generation. The Quaker concept of the total gospel necessitates a firm rejection of such immaturity.

4. *The fourth way in which the total gospel combines contrasting elements is that it is both worldly and unworldly at the same time.* Many people suppose that here we have contradictory features between which we are forced to choose, but all of our past experience denies that this is the case.

Christianity must always be worldly in the sense that it is concerned with infiltrating or penetrating the world. The Christian fellowship, according to its Lord and Commander-in-Chief, is meant to be both the salt of the earth (Matt. 5:13) and the light of the world (Matt. 5:14). It is meant to be like leaven which affects the entire lump. In one of the most striking of all the statements of Christ in regard to worldliness, we find Him saying that "the field is the world" (Matt. 13:38). The purpose of the Church is not to save itself, but to be a liberating and saving influence in the totality of civilization. Only as the Church loses itself, ceasing to be over-concerned with its own success, will it have the true success of changing the total culture.

Important as is the idea just explained, and deeply involved as it is in Christian philosophy, it must be balanced by the other side of the paradox, in that Christians must also live and think in contrast to the world. It is especially fallacious to think that Christians must go along with the popular naturalism which some Christian writers seem to think is the only way in which they can reach the ears of our generation. Indeed, we are more likely to affect the world if we are not identical with the world! We stand for a different discipline and for a more demanding way of life; we seek to obey orders which come from beyond the world. In short, the Christian is one who hears another drummer.

Quakerism involves an already verified philosophy. In one sense, it is the philosophy of pragmatism. We have learned that the only test of our apostleship is the difference we make. This is why we must stress, more and more, the identification of our religion with common life. There may be times when we ought to be in the cloister, but it is perfectly clear that the cloister is no place to *remain*. The only excuse for our separateness is our consequent effect on the totality of our culture.

We have a vivid example of the paradox of "unworldly worldliness" in the origin of the Peace Corps. Nearly all who know anything about it realize that the Peace Corps is essentially an extension of what had already been tried out in a host of Quaker work camps and foreign service deputations for several decades. Of course we are glad, because there is no compliment equal to the compliment of imitation. Instead of being possessive, we must rejoice when our dreams are borrowed and implemented beyond anything within our meager powers.

The clear lesson is that we must never rest, but proceed to inaugurate new chapters in the story of the infection of the world by an unworldly group. Consider, for example, the possibility of starting a new venture in creating opportunities for men and women who are able to qualify for early retirement. This has been part of our pattern in the past, perhaps the most brilliant example being that of Francis T. King, of Baltimore. Because Francis King was able to retire from business, he gave himself without stint to the creative work of rebuilding, in the American South, after the close of the Civil War. Life in some parts of the South, and particularly the Carolinas, is different to this day because of the work of Francis T. King and the Baltimore Association.

Notice that such a practice could be followed by many if only the idea were to be generally presented. Many do not really want to spend the rest of their lives playing shuffle-board, but the creative alternative of adult volunteer service has not occurred to them as a live option. It did occur to a contemporary Quaker physician, Dr. Herbert Bowles, of Honolulu. Consequently, he has ended his regular career and has now given a year in Newfoundland, as well as a subsequent year in West Africa. Why not? Why should not this become standard Christian practice? Why should we not make current the grand idea of a service chapter to follow the paid chapter of a busy man's life? Why should a man not retire early from industry and give himself to something even more creative?

This is only one possible illustration of the paradox of worldliness, but it is probably the one to stress now. My hope is that our American Friends Board of Missions, under the guidance of its new leader, Harold Smuck, will work seriously to develop a "guild of the economically liberated." If Quakers should give this dream practical embodiment for a few years it is not at all unlikely that it might later be taken up by the government, just as the Peace Corps has already been.

The best forces in the world work by beneficent contagion. They get something going which, at first, is hardly noticed, but later the contagion is widespread. Unworldly worldliness starts with little things, develops them so far as is possible, and then turns them loose to infect the world. Our task as Quakers, then, is the double task of building a spiritual laboratory where the experiments are conducted, and then giving the results to others in the hope they will borrow them. It will, I think, please you to know that I have had the opportunity to present vocally to the present President of the

United States the idea of a Liberated Corps. We do not know when the idea will take hold, but it will take hold faster if we make a laboratory test.

When we consider four features of a total Gospel, as we have now done, we have certainly not seen all that there is to see, but, if we mean what we say, we are saying something of extreme importance. The reason why I am a Quaker, as my fathers have been for so many generations, is that I am convinced that, in the idea of the total gospel, there is a vision without which the world will perish. Our concern, therefore, is not for ourselves but for mankind, for all who are made in God's image and for whom Christ died. I want the Quaker emphasis to continue, not for the sake of ourselves, but because it is an emphasis which is capable of overcoming some of the spiritual poverty of the world.

Chapter 8

Reality in Worship

My coming to North Carolina for this particular lecture is fundamentally an act of remembrance. Just forty years ago, this month, I began my teaching career and I have always been glad that I began it at Guilford. North Carolina, the land of my fathers, seemed to me then and seems to me now a very gracious part of this earth. The congregation of Friends at High Point has long been held by me in affection and admiration. I am especially glad that I was with you for the dedication of this beautiful structure in which we are now gathered. Forty years may not seem very long, in some ways, but it constitutes one eighth of the entire history of the Quaker Movement.

My purpose in this lecture is to deal as honestly and as thoroughly as I can with the strange human experience called worship. The subject is one which we shall never exhaust, because it has a magnitude denied to any other. Worship is the most ambitious of all of the enterprises in which human beings engage, because, while the mystery can be attacked at many points, in worship we seek direct contact with One who alone is ultimate. We sense the nobility of atomic research, and our imaginations are enlarged as we think of the possibility of human journeys to other planets, but these are as nothing compared with the simplest act of worship.

If, beyond all finite selves, and likewise beyond all finite things, there is the "Eternal Thou," whom men can know and

This lecture was delivered as the annual Quaker Lecture at High Point Monthly Meeting of Friends, High Point, North Carolina, in September of 1967.

love, and who can know and love us, that is tremendous news. All thoughtful persons are full of wonder as they pierce deeply into the secrets of created objects, but all of this is secondary in reference to the uncreated.

It is important to make abundantly clear that, when we speak of worship we refer, always, to a direct experience of The Living God. We do not refer to a mere subjective feeling in ourselves, but to a Divine-Human encounter. The whole subject is an idle one unless God really and objectively is. We are concerned with what is as truly objective as is a stone or a tree, but with characteristics which neither the stone nor the tree can have. We do not refer to some vague and abstract Ground of Being, but to the God of Abraham, Isaac and Jacob. We mean to speak of one who is truly and completely personal, as Christ was personal. If Christ is, as He reported, a true revelation of the Father, then there is no escape from the logical conclusion that God is a Person. Obviously, this does not mean that he is bodily, for this is not what we mean when we speak of ourselves as persons. We mean by person, a concrete center of consciousness and of self-consciousness. If God is less than this, religion is a waste of time and worship, as experienced at the deepest levels, is a snare and a delusion. By worship we mean a direct "meeting of minds," the mind of the finite person and the Mind of the Universal Person.

When we see worship in this exalted light we understand why we ought to tremble, either literally or figuratively, when we worship, because the undertaking is one of overwhelming magnitude. Though the nickname "Quaker" was first given us by our enemies in derision, it really represents a striking insight into the meaning of worship as a whole. Those who are not "tremblers" when they worship, demonstrate by their dullness and their calmness that they do not know what they are doing. The heresy is not that of those who *quake*, but of those who gather for worship lightly. We tremble because we come together, not to get money, or to instruct one another, but to be brought into a new experience of life and power, by direct acquaintance with the Living God. The most brilliant of all interpretations of the Quaker way of life included a statement which expressed the magnitude of worship in memorable words:

When assembled, the great work of one and all ought to be to wait upon God; and returning out of their own thoughts and imaginations to feel the Lord's presence, and know a gathering into his name indeed, where he is in the midst, according to his promise. And as every one is thus gathered, and so met together inwardly in their spirits, as well as outwardly in their persons, there the secret power and virtue of life is known to refresh the soul, and the pure motions and breathings of God's Spirit are felt to arise.[1]

If the eloquence of Barclay at the age of twenty-six astounds us, we have some explanation of it in the fact that he was speaking, not by speculation, but from firsthand experience. Especially did he know the sense of wonder which came to him and to his fellow prisoners in foul jails. The authorities could lock the doors, but they could not stop the encounter which made men tremble. That Barclay was by no means alone in what he reported is shown by the corroborating words of another prisoner, Isaac Penington:

This then is the way of worshipping in the true Light; diverse living stones meeting together, every one retiring in spirit into the living name, into the power which begat them, they all meet in one and the same place, in one and the same power, in one and the same fountain of Life; and here they bow down to tell the Father of life, offering up living sacrifices to him, and receiving the bread and water of life from him, and feeding in the rich pasture of his infinite fulness.[2]

What is surprising is not that some men and women should quake, but that any intelligent person can approach worship in any other way. The ultimate heresy is to make small what is intrinsically large. To look upon worship as a familiar routine of over-familiar phrases and postures is to be guilty of real blasphemy. It is as bad to approach God lightly as to approach Him empty.[3]

Religion is always shameful when it becomes an unexciting routine. This is almost inevitable when worship is identified with ritual. Whenever we think that saying words constitutes worship we are in manifest danger, for it is always possible to say words with no inner conviction. An atheist bishop can conduct the ritual as well as a believer, particularly if he is an

---

[1]Robert Barclay, *Apology*, XI, vi.
[2]Works of Isaac Penington, (2nd ed. London, 1761), Vol. I, p. 491.
[3]See Deuteronomy, 16:16.

accomplished actor. Religion is always in decay when it becomes a monopoly of a priestly class. Part of the danger lies in the fact that this kind of religion is so easy. It is not difficult to don vestments and learn to walk in a procession. But to mean what we say is always difficult. The prophets of Israel, in their continuous rejection of the identification of worship with ritual, were really crying out against the blasphemy of insincerity. This is why they rejected the emphasis upon new moons and sabbaths. The Temple *could* be a scene of real worship, but often it was an ostentatious alternative to reality. Thus Christ could say, "Something greater than the temple is here" (Matt. 12:6).

Because the dangers, even the Quaker dangers, are so obvious, we need to seek, again and again, to understand what the essence of worship really is. To paraphrase the Apostle Paul, it is neither ritual nor lack of ritual, but a new reality. Though bowing, kneeling and singing may be aids to worship, they, in themselves, are not worship at all. They are mere instruments. Always we must be on our guard against the identification of means and ends. All physical acts or sounds may profitably be compared to window glass. The purpose of glass in a window is not to exist for its own sake, but to let the light shine through. We are always on safe ground when we keep uppermost the demand for reality in contrast with anything artificial. The only reality is the "Real Presence." This is why the best loved of all Quaker paintings is called "The Presence in the Midst."

We are eternally grateful for the fact that the author of the Fourth Gospel preserved for posterity the story of Christ's encounter with the woman at the well of Samaria. What He said to the woman and, consequently to us, was that worship is always less than the best if it is dependent upon a special set of circumstances. The person who argues about whether true worship must be performed in this particular place or *that* one, is simply missing the point entirely. The only worship worth discussing is that which is in spirit and in truth. It is possible that we are too familiar with these hallowed words, and that new translations may be helpful. Perhaps a translation of the Greek words meaningful to modern man is: "True worship is *personal* and real." Personal is a word which gathers up the essence of "in spirit" while "real" is what we mean when we say "in truth." We are, that is, dealing with an experience which is, at once, intensely personal and absolutely genuine. It is a Person whom we meet and He is really here.

If we take Christ's words seriously, we soon realize that the heart of genuine worship is prayer. It is not mere meditation, for meditation can be self-centered, whereas prayer is necessarily God-centered. In prayer we respond directly to God in recognition of His seeking us. What a great idea it is that He seeketh us to worship Him! In short, however dull we may be, He does not leave us alone. But the correspondence, in order to be real, must be reciprocal. The central wonder is that of the double search.

A religion without prayer is not a religion worth having. If we did not know this already we should know it from the observation that Christ prayed. But how shall we pray? Shall it be together or alone? A curious idea has developed, to the effect that we must choose between these, and that Christ decided for us by saying "When you pray, go into your room and pray alone." The repetition of these words has seemed to some to be an adequate refutation of the idea that Christians ought to pray together. What such people miss is that Christ made more than one reference to prayer and that, by His own example, he demonstrated the variety which is right and proper. That He joined in group prayer, which is worship at its best, is shown by the story of the Mount of Transfiguration. There He certainly prayed, but there He was not in His closet. The only rational conclusion is that there are times to pray alone, and that there are times to pray in the company of others. No doubt Christ was referring to a special need in a particular situation when, in the Sermon on the Mount, He advocated aloneness.

Normally we need one another in life, and this is especially true in the act of worship. The ancient truth is that iron sharpens iron (Proverbs 27:17). The irons, we recognize in our humility, may be of poor stuff, but God can use even base metals for His glory. The poor man who sits in worship with his face aglow might suppose that he is helping nobody and yet be extremely helpful to those who watch him. The very act of seeing the faces of others may be a means of growth and power. Rocks may not need other rocks, but it is the nature of spirits or persons to need each other.

One problem which arises today, even more than formerly, is that of the necessity of special times and places of worship. A great many now reject worship at a particular hour because, they say, they are able to worship in all kinds of times. This sounds very noble, but actually is not. Indeed, it is a striking example of a phony spirituality. Early Friends had to face this danger, particularly in the influence of John Perrot, who was most damaging in colonial Virginia. The trouble with the hyper-spiritual approach is that it is fundamentally self-centered. To claim to be sufficient is to lack both humility and intellectual honesty. However spiritual I am, I am not really self-sufficient, and I need the help which others can give me. Furthermore, I may, unworthy as I am, help them. The person, then, who absents himself from public worship because his private worship is alleged to be sufficient, is not even asking the right question. The deepest question is not "What do I personally need or enjoy?" but "What is required of me as a follower of Christ?"

The truth is that continual prayer and especially arranged prayer are not incompatible. There is a time for both. We soon notice that those who are most faithful in the group encounter are precisely those who have the most continuous sense of the Presence in their everyday lives. Fortunately, this is not a problem in which choice is needed.

There is no conflict between the idea that God is in all places and that He is in some places. He is in a barn as truly as He is in the Taj Mahal, but, given our finitude, there is a vast difference between our ability to recognize Him in different settings. This is why there is nothing wrong about constructing a building in which the physical setting is conducive to worship. God does not dwell exclusively in buildings made with hands, but it may be easier to recognize Him in some such buildings than in others. What we must always oppose, of course, is the pre-Christian idea that God is more in an altar than in a factory. Christ cannot be carried around in a chalice. He is in the water which quenches thirst as truly as He is in the holy water which has been blessed.

It is primarily because of the wonder of our undertaking that there must always be preparation for worship. Though God is seeking us, we must not expect magic. The right approach is to come together with our hearts and minds full to overflowing. The terrible heresy of many alleged worshippers is that they make no effort to get ready. People who would not think of visiting an art gallery without some preparation and some thought about what to expect, gather for worship with no advance effort at all. How different it is for those who, if they are to worship on Sunday, make it a practice to avoid Saturday night social engagements. This leaves them precious time in which to study passages of Scripture, to pray alone, to think quietly and thus to get ready for the stupendous event. The strange fact is that this practice is really rare and would seem to some to be somewhat bizarre. What is really bizarre is to appear before God empty and unprepared. Just as the serious surgeon gets ready for the operation and the serious professor gets ready for his lecture, so the serious worshipper must get ready for the divine revelation which he expects.

Since truth comes to us primarily in paradox, we must expect a paradox in connection with worship. For worship to be real we must not only be prepared; we must also be *open*. On the surface the two requirements seem to be in conflict. If I am prepared, will I not then proceed, as I have planned, especially in uttering words which may be given to me in advance? But to be open means that there may be genuine surprises and that I must expect the unexpected. The important observation is that the contrasting features of preparation and openness or freedom are both needed and that, in actual experience, they are by no means incompatible, though different. We must work as though all depends on God. We must get ready with the integrity of intellectual toil, and then be willing to forget everything originally planned, if clear leading points in a different direction.

The central paradox of worship is beautifully expressed in some inspired words of Lewis Wadilove, the English Friend who was chairman of the Fourth World Conference of Friends, so recently concluded. His formula was to have "a minimum of planning and a maximum of preparation." In regard to our ministry there is every reason why we should prepare, and to fail to do so stems more from laziness than spirituality. But it is a horrible mistake to go forward with what has been prepared, regardless of changing circumstances. It is the mind with the fullest preparation that can be the most flexible in the end.

As Quakers, we have some things for which we are rightly grateful, but we also have much for which we ought to be ashamed. One of the points of shame is that fact that worship, which ought to be our noblest effort, has come to be the subject of our most bitter division. Indeed, we are much more divided on worship than we are on points of theology. One group speaks proudly of worship on the basis of silence while the other speaks proudly of programmed worship. Sometimes there is even a spirit of mutual condescension. In my boyhood I often heard the two groups referred to, contemptuously, as "Slow Quakers" and "Fast Quakers."

What we need to make clear is that this division is absolutely unnecessary and that it would disappear if we were to think more carefully and to judge one another more compassionately. Each group has been right in what it has affirmed and wrong in what it has denied. Those who speak of "silent" worship are right in stressing the degree to which we ought to be open, and those who speak of "programmed" worship are right in stressing the degree to which we ought to be prepared. How strange that anyone should assume the necessity of an exclusive choice!

The language we have used has been a foolishly constructed barrier and this applies to both sides. It is clearly a mistake to speak of worshipping on the "basis of silence," for this is mere negativity. We could be silent and not care at all about the Presence of Christ in our midst. There is a silence which opens the door of wonder, but there is also another silence which is a thin cloak for lassitude and sleepiness. If we are honest we admit that there is a great deal of the latter.

On the other hand, it is a mistake to speak of "programmed" worship. The difficulty here is that the very language is offensive in that it smacks of human planning without sensitivity. Fortunately, for three hundred years, the best minds in the Quaker Movement have recognized that there is a better way than either silence or program. The better way is to come together with our hearts and minds full and then to be obedient. Certainly God can lead us on Tuesday as well as on Sunday, but on both Tuesday and Sunday we must beware of doing anything merely in our power and wisdom.

Robert Barclay proved himself our intellectual as well as spiritual leader when he pointed us to a deeper basis of worship which, had it been followed faithfully, would have precluded our unfortunate divisions. The great passage says that "as our worship consists not in words, so neither in silence, as silence, but in holy dependence of the mind upon God."[4] What a wonderful thing it would be if we, in the last third of the twentieth century, could recover and demonstrate this noble conception. Then, when we are asked how we worship, we could always say, "We worship on the basis of holy dependence."

Would you worship in a way that is personal and real? Then keep asking, day after day, but even more when you gather with others for worship, "Lord, what do you have to say to me?" Sometimes you will get an answer, and then the whole transaction becomes real.

[4]*Apology,* XI, ix.

Chapter 9

The Two-fold Secret of John Woolman

I am very conscious that this is Pentecost. The parable of the valley of dry bones in Ezekiel (which had been read during the service) is in many ways a prototype of Pentecost. It is the story of new life arising, and in this case arising paradoxically in a most unlikely place and fashion. This is the story of renewal. In our own generation, in this century, the renewal movement has undoubtedly been the most striking movement in Christianity — much more striking in the long run than the movement for church union. The movement for church union, as you know, has not been wholly successful. But the renewal movement has been wide-spread and significant. Even the Vatican Council, which was called the Ecumenical Council, was not really concerned with union but with renewal. This has appeared among Roman Catholics and all kinds of Protestants, and I am sure you feel it very keenly in this place.

This is really the theme of Pentecost. New life has arisen over and over in the history of our faith. Often when everything has been dark there has been a bright new light. I know that some of you are Methodists. How it must please you to think of what occurred in the eighteenth century, when it was confidently said by many philosophers that the Christian faith was over — that it was only a matter of burying the dead! And then in the north end of Lincolnshire, in a most unlikely

This address was presented in Great St. Mary's, the University Church of Cambridge, England, in May of 1972. This is the only message in this volume that was not presented to a specifically Quaker gathering. However, since the lecture deals with such a giant Quaker historical figure, and a man who has deeply touched the life of Elton Trueblood, I feel that its inclusion in this volume is justified.

101

village, the village of Epworth, there arose the remarkable Wesley family. On May 24, 1738, John Wesley walked into the Aldersgate Meeting House in London and heard a man reading the preface to Luther's *Commentary* on the Epistle to the Romans. One would not suppose that this was particularly inspiring, but it brought an utter change in Wesley's life, and all of you know his famous sentence, "My heart was strangely warmed." As a result of that, there came new life within the Church in far-flung places all around the world, because one man was made different. And so on Wednesday (May 24) I shall be in London and I shall walk up Aldersgate Street and stand for a little while where the meeting house once stood, and think not merely of what happened more than two hundred years ago but of what could happen now if we would meet the conditions of renewal.

Renewal is the very mark of vitality, but it does not come automatically. It does not come unless we meet the conditions. What are the conditions which you and I can fulfil if we are willing to do so? I think in this we can be helped by some very great models. I am thinking of a contemporary of John Wesley, whose name was John Woolman. . .I mention him partly because he, as one of the best known Quakers who ever lived, has touched my life very deeply. He made his one and only trip to England two hundred years ago. He was not famous then at all as he is now, when his *Journal* has been read by hundreds of thousands. Then, he was a very modest man from New Jersey. He was born in 1720 and he died in the city of York two hundred years ago, in 1772. In many places, especially in this country, much thought is being given to his life this summer. He grew up in such a modest way. He had a small business, and when he saw that the business was occupying too much of his time he began to suggest to his customers that they go to his competitors. He did not want his life to be cluttered with over-much business; and as he meditated he began to see a very great evil — the evil of slavery. When he was a young man, people were still bought and sold in most parts of the world. He wrote the first sizeable book on slavery as an unchristian thing. He made two great journeys in his ministry to the southern colonies, once when he was only 25 and then again when he was 36 years of age.

Wherever he went, he very tenderly showed people what it meant to buy and sell other human beings, because he saw they were made in the image of God, and people for whom Christ died. He went to the very community where my people lived in Carolina, and it is a striking thing to me to look at the record of my own family and to see that after Woolman's second visit to Carolina my great-great-grandfather liberated all his slaves. Not for any economic reasons, for it was most uneconomic. Certainly not for political reasons, but for the love of Christ and the consequent love of those whom Christ loves.

When Woolman was a little older, he felt strongly that he ought to visit England. . .When he got to London he decided, after one week, to move on towards the north. But he found out that the horses were overdriven on the stage coaches. . .He said: "I will not purchase my own comfort at such a price, the price of harm to God's creatures." And so he walked. He walked by a circuitous route all the way from London to York. When he got to York he caught smallpox and died. He was 51 years of age. . . .

I bring John Woolman to you when I am talking about renewal because he made a tremendous difference. And I have asked myself how such a modest man could do it. What was his secret? It was two-fold. In the first place, he had a very tender sense of all suffering, so that all suffering of any of God's creatures, and particularly of his fellow men, touched him very deeply — whatever their colour, whatever their nation, whatever their location. In the second place, his faith was deeply Christ-centered, so that he had a strong basis of inner power.

You might like to hear something that he said, especially when he was a very young man — not much older than the students of Cambridge University now.

> I saw in slavery so many vices and corruptions increased by trade and this way of life that it appeared to me as a dark, gloomy mass, hanging over the land, and though now many willingly run into it, yet in the future the consequences will be grievous. . . .

How marvellously true! How this has been verified! So many of our troubles in our generation have come as the moral consequences of a way of life in which people did not sufficiently feel the sufferings of others. When he was in the North of England he had a few days to write, and in his *Journal* he reported an experience that had come a little earlier.

> I was brought so near the gates of death that I forgot my name. Being then desirous to know who I was, I saw a mass of matter of a dull gloomy colour between the South and the East, and was informed that this mass was human beings in as great misery as they could be and live, and that I was mixed with them, and that henceforth I might not consider myself as a distinct and separate being. In this state I remained several hours. I then heard a soft, melodious voice, more pure and harmonious than any voice I had heard with my ears before; and I believed it was the voice of an angel who spake to the other angels. The words were: "John Woolman is dead." I soon remembered that I was once John Woolman and, being assured that I was alive in the body, I greatly wondered what that heavenly voice could mean. . .Then the mystery was opened, and I perceived there was joy in heaven over a sinner who had repented, and that that language, "John Woolman was dead," meant no more than the death of my own will.

I have been greatly moved by a prayer of John Woolman's which you might like to hear. It shows us something of the secret of the power of new life that came into him.

> O Lord my God! the amazing horrors of darkness were gathered round me and covered me all over and I saw no way to go forth. I felt the depth and extent of the misery of my fellow creatures, separated from the divine harmony; and it was heavier than I could bear, and I was crushed down under it. I lifted up my hand and stretched out my arms but there was none to help me; I looked round about, and was amazed at the depth of misery. O Lord! I remembered that thou art omnipotent; that I had called thee Father and I felt that I loved thee; and I was made quiet in thy will, and I waited for deliverance from thee; Thou hadst pity on me when no man could help me; I saw that meekness under suffering was showed unto us in the most effective example of thy son, and thou wast teaching me to follow him; and I said, thy will, O Father, be done.

These are some of the most vivid examples of his sense of the suffering, the pain, the anguish of human beings in so many parts of the world and in so many generations. And this is one side of the secret. But if he had had only the sense of suffering, without a real answer, it might have been a mere frustration. At the depth of his experience he was a completely Christ-centred man. So on the day that he died in York, just before his death, he asked for pen and paper. This is what he said:

> I believe my being here is in the wisdom of Christ. I know not as to life or death.

The last words that he spoke audibly were these:

> My dependance is in the Lord Jesus Christ, who I trust will forgive my sins, which is all I hope for; and if it be his will to raise up this body again, I am content; and if to die, I am resigned.

Now the relevance of this to our time is tremendous. As I go about among many kinds of Christians in the world, I am frequently saddened when I see the way in which we are polarised; often there is a great division between the people on the one side who are concerned with social action, and nothing but social action, and the people on the other side who are concerned with the development of the inner life of prayer and of worship and devotion, and nothing but that. I soon see that each of these alone is insufficient, for both are necessary.

The wonderful thing about Woolman is that he demonstrated the two sides in equal strength. He had a sense of the reality of the presence of the living Christ in his life; and the risen Christ with him, guiding him, leading him, and about this he was utterly unapologetic. He had a centre to his life: he had an alternative to confusion and to despair. On the other side, he had a tremendous concern for the overcoming of injustice wherever it might be found and the healing of wounds wherever they might be felt. If he had had only the inner life of devotion, without the social concern, it could have been self-centred. If he had had only the outer life of action without the inner spirit, it could have become harsh, judgmental and violent. But if the two can be held together, as they were perfectly together in Woolman's case, then we have the secret of Christian power.

What is required is the combination of roots and fruits. The roots alone do nothing; the fruits alone wither and die; but if the totality can be kept, then power emerges. I believe that this could be one of the greatest eras in the history of the Christian Church. The people who call this the post-Christian age will be proved wrong as all their predecessors have been. Christ said of the Church, "The powers of death will not be able to prevail against it," and I believe that. I think it will go on, but it will only be able to go on because humble people like ourselves will find something like the combination which the modest tailor of New Jersey found two hundred years ago. There may be other conditions of renewal, but these are obvious — a great tenderness towards all human suffering and a centring on Jesus Christ which will give us stability and power.

Chapter 10

The Contribution of Quakerism to the Recovery of Vital Christianity

There are many things required of us today, but the first requirement is what may be termed "sanctified thinking." We cannot play our proper role merely by going on as we are, doing uncritically each year what has been done in the recent past. Because the danger of moral and spiritual decay is very great, we cannot rightly face this danger without an agonizing reappraisal of our position in the world. Somewhat as Barclay and Penn thought rigorously about the Quaker contribution three hundred years ago, we must use our best resources to think about it now.

The fact that we have survived three hundred twenty years is no guarantee of continued survival. Many movements, especially religious movements, have flourished for a while and then have disappeared, almost without a trace. Some of the developments which have terminated have been Quaker ones. For example, there was formed, in 1853, a group called "Progressive Friends," centered in the general area of Kennet Square, Pennsylvania. They were social activists, strongly anti-slavery and, for a few decades, marked by genuine vigor. Indeed, they had sufficient vigor to arrange a deputation to visit President Lincoln in the White House in the darkest year of the Civil War, 1862. These people were well received by Lincoln, who listened courteously to their appeal for an Emancipation Proclamation. A few weeks after their visit he wrote the first draft of his own Proclamation. But, able and

This message was delivered as the annual Quaker Lecture, at the 1972 sessions of Indiana Yearly Meeting.

107

dedicated as these "Progressive Friends" were, they lost their enthusiasm and finally disbanded in the earlier part of our own century, having existed as a conscious religious body less than a century.

Another vivid example of decline is that provided by the Shakers. Starting two hundred years ago, they established strong communities in areas as far apart as New England and Kentucky. They, like the Progressive Friends, were especially strong just prior to the period of the Civil War. Now, though their memory is widely honored, these saintly people have little more than historical significance. A very few old people still live as Shakers in Maine and New Hampshire, but the power departed long ago. Fortunately, the Kentucky community, south of Lexington, is now the scene of a concerted effort devoted to Christian Renewal, but that is another story, altogether. As we look at the diaries of the last of the faithful brothers and sisters, we can sense their deep sadness as they recognized that they were part of something which, though once powerful, was losing its vitality every day. They exhibited all the familiar pathos of supporters of a lost cause.

A third significant example of a once vital but finally obsolete cause is that of the Catholic Apostolic Church. This was founded in 1835, partly as a result of the influence of Edward Irving, who died in 1834. In consequence, the members were popularly called "Irvingites." These people had great vitality, sometimes spoke with tongues, expected the Second Coming at any moment, and demonstrated a variety of spiritual gifts. Twelve members were set aside as Apostles, but the last of these died in 1901, and there has been no continuation of such leadership. The fine building erected by the church, at Gordon Square, London, has now been turned over to the Church of England. A few members survive, but only as a remnant. It is a sad ending of what was once bold and vigorous. We are bound to wonder if our Quaker history may end in an equally pathetic fashion.

The important truth to face now is that Quakerism will become one of the lost causes unless we make now the moves which can lead to renewed vitality. The paradoxical insight which has come to me in this regard is that we shall not endure by giving our main attention to what is good for the Religious Society of Friends, but rather to what is good for the world. In short, our concern must be more ecumenical than sectarian.

We should try to exist, I believe, not for our own sakes, and not because we take pride in our particular heritage, but because we are needed. In this, and only in this, is there any possible justification of continued existence. The nurture of a little ingrown sect is a matter of very small business and one emphatically not worth the trouble. If Quakerism becomes an ingrown movement, obsessed with itself, it will die. *Our only hope lies in a sense of mission for the sake of the world.*

The New Ecumenicity is one of the really encouraging developments of our troubled century. In the contemporary world there is not much interest, any more, in trying to create a single monolithic church, but there is great interest in a mutuality of sharing among separate bodies, each with something to contribute to all of the others. The chief features of this ideal were already clear in 1948 when we met at Amsterdam to establish the World Council of Churches. We were encouraged to create, not union, but unity, in a fellowship of Christians, humble enough to learn from one another and courageous enough to share our treasures. In line with this truly noble pattern, the conduct of morning worship each day during the Assembly was allocated to one of the separate bodies. Thus there was a Lutheran service one morning, an Anglican Morning Prayer on another, and so on. To our delight we, as Quakers, were asked to arrange a period of Quaker worship on Saturday morning. Fortunately, this worship, shared by at least six hundred persons, was one of the high points of a week memorable in Christian history.

The ideal of reverent sharing applies to the relationships between the various branches of Quakerdom. Just as it is not required of us that we exalt Quakerism, so it is not required that we exalt any one branch of the Quaker Movement. We engage in different practices in various parts of the world, but this, of itself, is neither surprising nor damaging. Though outside observers often profess to be shocked by our Quaker variety there is no good reason why uniformity should be demonstrated. Indeed, richness comes by variety, and variety is not harmful providing there is mutual humility. On the whole, it is a good thing that some groups of Friends gather with advance planning while others gather without such planning, for each has something valuable to give to the other. The highest ecumenical ideal is that in which each contributes its best to the whole without claiming to have a monopoly on either truth or virtue. One of our greatest dangers is that according to which each branch of our Quaker family tends to become a sect within a sect. Unfortunately, this has, to some extent, already occurred. One evidence is that, for the most part, those who read *The Friends Journal* have practically no acquaintance with those who read *Quaker Life* and vice versa.

Though there are a few bright spots in contemporary Christendom, there is also a vast amount of gloom. On every side we hear of growing apathy and of dying congregations. Many report a shocking failure to reach the young. The efforts in which some engage to revive interest are often little more than new evidences of decay. What is offered, frequently, is more recreation, when what is needed is conviction. The trouble with many of our churches is not a lack of organizations or absence of buildings or even of novel programs, but the decline of strong belief. Unless there can be a robust recovery of belief in the modern world we are not likely to see recovery in other ways. We know that renewal is possible, since it has come in dark times before, but it does not come unless the conditions are met. If we believe, as I do, that a vital Christianity is what the modern world most needs, we must give our best thinking to the examination of ways in which its recovery may take place.

We have made a strong start on our agonizing reappraisal of our place in the world when we become clear about our purpose. Since our intention is not to exalt Quakerism, but rather to enlarge and enrich the Kingdom of Christ, our function is to examine what we have learned in three centuries of experience and to try to make it available to our fellow Christians of all denominations. We must avoid, if we can, the temptation to speak exclusively to and with Friends. We must speak with others more often than with ourselves, seeking to learn what they have to teach us, because we need all of the help which we can get. At the same time we must tell with boldness anything we know which is too valuable to hug to our own bosoms.

Among the many possible contributions which Friends can make, there are now three which seem to be of supreme value. Though these are in no sense our private monopoly, each being already shared by others to some degree, it is nevertheless true that Friends have emphasized each of these in a peculiar manner.

(1) The first important contribution of Friends to the Recovery of Christian Vitality is the combination of inner life and outer service. So close has this connection been that it is hard to say which of the two aspects has been most notable. On the one hand, Friends have been well known for successive chapters of Practical Christianity. The story of social and moral pioneering is always a thrilling one. In wave after wave of creative imagination, Friends have seen the possibility of attacking a series of entrenched evils. The most conspicuous of these have been the recognition of the sin of human slavery, the effort to treat the mentally ill without cruelty, the change in ideas about prisoners, and the long effort to engage in peacemaking. Successive Quaker generations have been able to engage in new forms of social action, each of these being motivated by the desire to set God's children free from all that holds them back from fullness of life. This is a heritage in which we rightly take satisfaction and which we must try to continue in our own generation.

At the same time that Friends have been known for dramatic attacks upon various forms of oppression, they have been equally known for the cultivation of the inner life of devotion. Those who suppose that the Society of Friends is merely a humanitarian society demonstrate a surprising ignorance of history. The stress on waiting before God has been quite as great as has been the stress on the performance of human service. No group of people in the world has been as much given to the keeping of Journals, most of them emphasizing the reality of the Divine Encounter. William Penn is, of course, known for his work as a colonist, establishing what he called "An Holy Experiment in Government," but he is also known as the author of *No Cross No Crown* and *Fruits of Solitude*.

It is something of a revelation to note the high standing of

Quaker accounts of the Spiritual Life among the acknowledged classics of devotion. At least three, written by Friends, are often included in modern lists of devotional classics. These are John Woolman's *Journal, The Christian's Secret of a Happy Life,* by Hannah Whitall Smith, and *Testament of Devotion,* by Thomas Kelly. When we think how few in number the really great devotional books are, it is obvious that we are represented in a fashion radically disproportionate to our numbers.

The three books just mentioned do not, by any means, exhaust the Quaker contribution, but they are especially significant for the way in which they have affected Christian readers who though they have no connection with the Quaker Movement, are grateful for the help provided. In all three cases the readers outside our borders far outnumber the readers inside. How striking to realize, for example, that *The Christian's Secret of a Happy Life* has actually been purchased by more than two million readers. Only a tiny minority of these readers have been members of the Religious Society of Friends, but this is as it should be.

Other Quakers who have helped mightily in strengthening the interior life are Isaac Penington, in the seventeenth century, and Rufus M. Jones in modern times. In most of his fifty-six books, Dr. Jones sought to explore and enrich the life within. This was what he termed his "life clue." In our own generation there has appeared a renewed interest in the study of the often obscure Journals in which modest men tell others of the ways in which God has reached them.

The chief message in this connection which Friends are able to give to the world is that the two enterprises not only *can* go together, but *must* go together. Far from being incompatible, they are necessary for each other. If we have only the cultivation of the inner life, without social action, we become self-centered and complacent. On the other hand, if we have only social action without the tenderness which comes from within, we become arrogant, judgmental, and sometimes violent in our protests. The only hope lies in holding the roots and the fruits together. If either one is absent, death is certain to ensue. In some places such death has already occurred.

The example of John Woolman provides us with the classic

Quaker pattern which we should be glad to emulate. As we look at Woolman's remarkable life it is difficult to know in which of the two areas his greatest contribution lies. On the one hand, he was amazingly effective in regard to the evils of slavery, war, and poverty. He saw, with a clarity seldom vouchsafed to any before him, that it is a wicked thing to buy, sell, and own other human beings. But even the cursory reader of his *Journal* is aware that he was not primarily an abolitionist. There was almost nothing in common between Woolman and John Brown. His tenderness included the slave owner as well as the slave, and this tenderness came from a deep place. He wanted to liberate the slave because the slave, like himself, was one for whom Christ died. It was out of his regular practice of both private and shared worship that there came his revolutionary insights about economic and social life. There is not likely to be any genuine renewal of Christianity anywhere, unless the Woolman pattern is adopted with serious conviction.

(2) The second contribution which Friends can make to a world willing to listen is another combination, that which we may term Rational Evangelicalism. On all sides we find Christians who are failing to produce conviction because they stress only one side of the necessary combination of the warm heart and the clear head. There are, on the one hand, numerous congregations in which there is undoubtedly genuine emphasis on a Christ-centered faith, but, because this faith is not presented with cogency, it is not really heard by the people who try to be intellectually honest, but make little redemptive impact because they have no firm center of reference.

It is important to remember that Quakerism, in its main historic stream, has been both evangelical and rational. It has been evangelical in the sense that it has been truly Christ-centered; it has been rational in the sense that it has sought to give to all who will listen a reasonable account of the hope by which we are sustained. The most successful examplar of this combination in Quaker history was Robert Barclay (1648-1690). Part of our good fortune is that Barclay's famous book, *The Apology,* has been more widely distributed than any other book dealing with the Christian faith as espoused by Friends.

There is, today, danger on both sides, that of a loss of

intelligibility and that of a loss of a firm center of conviction, but the latter is the more serious of the present dangers. Quakerism is, in some areas, being watered down so that it is little more than a vague humanism, with no firm center of reference. Even when the name of God is used, as it often is not, the most that is allowed is the overworked cliche, "that of God in every man." Since this is often used with no reference to Christ, it is not surprising when strangers conclude that the Quaker faith is something quite outside the Christian faith.

One effective solution to this problem is a closer attention to the words and convictions of our founders, and particularly those of George Fox. Fox did not begin with humanism, as something to be understood apart from dependence upon the Divine Source. Certainly he was not operating in his own power. Far more revelatory than his oblique reference to "that of God" in man, was his forthright conviction about the sufficiency of Jesus Christ. His real conversion began, not with reference to God in general, but with reference to Christ in particular. "There is one, even Christ Jesus," said the inner voice, "that can speak to thy condition." The people who neglect this specific reference may personally be good people, but they are promoting something radically different from the Basic Christianity which changed the life of Fox and, through him, the lives of so many more.

There is no doubt that the faith of the first generation of Friends was radically Christ-centered and not some kind of religion in general. Fox is reported to have said, "I took men to Jesus Christ and left them there," and his closest associates felt the same way. Barclay, of course, was unequivocal in this regard. "Our great and chiefest work," he wrote, "is and ought to be communion with Christ." It was this kind of definite faith which made it possible for Quakers to grow with speed in forty years of amazing vitality.

The evangelical stance of John Woolman was equally clear, up to the very end of his life. In his final illness, at York, his companions heard the sick man say, "My dependence is in the Lord Jesus Christ, who I trust will forgive my Sins, which is all I hope for; and if it be his Will to raise up this Body again, I am content; and if to die, I am resigned." After this, Woolman could not speak audibly any more, but he asked for pen and ink and wrote as his final words, "I believe my being here is in the Wisdom of Christ; I know not as to Life or Death." He did not claim to know everything, but he knew *something*, and one thing was sufficient.

The renewal of Quaker vitality in the great burst of energy connected, at the beginning of our own century, with the work of John Wilhelm Rowntree, represented no diminution of the Quaker emphasis on Christ as the Center. What Rowntree is most remembered for is a prayer, and it is good to notice its specific words: "Thou, O Christ, Convince us by thy spirit."

If this kind of commitment can be combined with fearless examination of all aspects of truth that are available to us, we have an unbeatable combination. There is no incompatibility between such firmness at the Center and exploration at the edges. The Christ-centered person can and should be open to any developments which natural science, in any of its branches, can provide. The true evangelical is scientifically minded, because he is not afraid of any possible disclosures that will undermine his faith. He has no need to retreat for safety into some theological shell, because his central faith makes him intellectually bold. If we have only evangelicalism, without rational inquiry, we become exclusive and sectarian. If we have rational inquiry, without a firm center of conviction, we are bound to end in confusion. It is important to know that it is the people who are both Christ-centered and rational who are the ones now making the most difference in the modern world. This is because they are free from sectarianism of either the right or the left. To be sectarian is to attach one's self to a "section" rather than to seek for wholeness.

Because Quakers have an honorable history in combining intellect and spirituality, they have a message for the world. A long line of Quakers, starting with Robert Barclay in the seventeenth century and continuing to our own, prove that the combination is possible. Our message to the world is that the combination is not only possible, but crucially necessary.

(3) The third contribution which Quakerism can make to world Christianity concerns the Christian Ministry. One of the most striking facts of Quakerism, in its revolutionary early period, was the impression that all Friends were engaged in the ministry. "By a living ministry," wrote Penn, "at first we were

reached and turned to the Truth." When Robert Fowler, in his famous account of the voyage of the *Woodhouse,* mentioned the passengers, he referred to all of them as "the ministers of Christ." It was *because* they were ministers that "they gathered sticks and kindled a fire and left it burning." Worship is important, early Friends discovered, but Ministry is even more important because it is potentially continuous, wherever there are people.

Others besides ourselves have, especially in the recent past, encouraged what is termed the "lay ministry," but Friends have gone farther with stress upon the "universal ministry." What we have to tell the world is that a Christian and a minister are synonymous terms. Of course, we have not demonstrated this pattern in a perfect manner, but, in our best periods, the exciting pattern has always been implicit. The ministry, we hold, cannot be delegated to a clerical class of men, the rest of us feeling a consequent freedom from responsibility. Christ, when He calls us, calls us, not to be His admirers, but His fellow workers. This is the obvious meaning of His yoke, a meaning which Quakers have helped to clarify in our particular generation.

Fortunately, the message to the world about the possibility of a universal Christian ministry is in no way incompatible with the recognition of a variety of gifts. The gifts of the scholarly Isaac Penington were not identical with those of the rough countryman, Edward Burrough. There is, of course, no good reason for uniformity in the ministry. In the eighteenth century John Woolman and other persons, both male and female, who travelled as he did were referred to as "Public Friends." They had a very special ministry, that of reaching strangers in a great variety of locations. In Woolman's last journey, that to England exactly 200 years ago, his life touched the lives of many other Public Friends. He knew the importance of the travelling ministry in stirring up the ministry of those who are unable to travel. After he had reached York and enjoyed some freedom to write at the home of George and Jane Crosfield, he produced, as his last serious writing, an essay: "Concerning the Ministry," thus indicating where his consuming interest lay. In the midst of this appeared the following striking passage:

Oh! how deep is Divine wisdom! Christ puts forth his ministers, and goeth before them; and Oh! how great is the danger of departing from the pure feeling of that which leadeth safely!

Christ knoweth the state of the people, and in the pure feeling of the gospel ministry, their states are opened to his servants.

Christ knoweth when the fruit-bearing branches themselves have need of purging.

One message which Friends can share with the Church Universal is that there are not two kinds of Christians, clergy and laity, but hundreds of kinds. Since ministry is so rich that it is by no means limited to public speaking, there may, actually, be as many kinds of ministry as there are persons.

Our ancestors, when they created the pastoral system a century ago, had in mind the earlier pattern of Public Friends. On paper the only novelty was that of establishing such persons in permanent residence. For the most part, those called pastors ceased to be itinerants and settled down to the task of trying to stir up new life in particular localities. There is no good reason to suppose that the new emphasis was, in general, a mistake, but we can now see that a mistake was made in one particular aspect, that of taking over the conventional Protestant pattern of clerical status and grafting it on to the Quaker plant. Without meaning to do so, the initiators of the pastoral system made a radical alteration in Quaker history, the most serious and damaging change being that many of the rank and file were led, in consequence, to feel a sharp diminution in responsibility. There came a growing tendency to leave all of the preaching and visiting to a man hired for the purpose, thus reintroducing some of the worst features of the "hireling ministry" which George Fox had so vigorously opposed.

The time came, as we all know, when the lives of some Public Friends, liberated from secular earning, came to be essentially identical with those of neighboring clergymen. Ultimately Quaker pastors were freely addressed with the title "Reverend," and were listed, along with the clergy, in telephone directories. This practice continues to occur in some areas, even today, in spite of the strong revulsion which has set in against such practices.

It is possible to make a rational defense of a Quaker pastoral system provided the pastor is seen, not as a person with clerical status, but as one minister among others who is liberated financially in order to stir up the ministry of his brethren. Here is a pattern which Christians, in most bodies, have not even imagined as possible. It can make the best of both worlds, provided it is demonstrated with a clear understanding of its dangers. The Quaker conviction, which we must share with the world, is that the *laity can be abolished.* But it cannot be abolished unless there are men and women who are dedicated to its abolition. The great new idea which, though not confined to Friends, is now more clearly envisaged by them than by any other group, is that the "Equipping Ministry" is the key to renewal. Unless we employ this key, many doors will remain locked.

Personally, I am very glad that I am a Quaker. I am glad, not because I think Friends have the whole truth about anything, but because Friends hold certain treasures which are required if Christian Renewal is to occur on any significant scale. The Renewal Movement is the most notable single development of our century, so far as the Christian Faith is concerned. There is, of course, apathy and decay in many quarters, but the exciting fact is that the lesson of the Parable of the Valley of Dry Bones (Ezekiel 37:1-14) is now believed by representatives of many different branches of the Church of Christ. It is thrilling to recognize the new life that is emerging in the very presence of death, but it is even more thrilling to be a part of this widespread renewal. My strongest reason for remaining a Quaker, in spite of many reasons for discouragement, is that Quakers can participate in the new life that is emerging. My prayer is that we shall be faithful!

Chapter 11

The Quaker Vision

We emerged as a people before we had a name. In the subsequent three hundred twenty-five years, we have had many different names, but none has ever been fully satisfactory. The most widely accepted name, "Quakers," came originally, not from ourselves, but from our enemies and detractors. It has, no doubt, been a wise step to take what has been thus given and seek to make it meaningful. This was the strategy of the two chief intellectuals of our movement in the seventeenth century, Robert Barclay and William Penn. Both sought to take what was used in scorn and to glorify it. Thus the young Barclay entitled the most famous of all of our books *An Apology for the True Christian Divinity, as the same is held forth and preached by the people, called, in scorn Quakers.* Eighteen years later, William Penn accepted the same challenge when he had the opportunity to write his Introduction to the handsome edition of the *Journal* of George Fox which was published in honor of the founder in 1694, after being edited by Thomas Ellwood. Penn deliberately made his introduction a major literary production, worthy of being published separately, and gave it a separate title. He called it "The Rise and Progress of the People Called Quakers," thereby giving support to the usage already practiced by others. The sensitive reader will note the use of the term "people." Before we had a name we were, indeed, a people.

Barclay's account of the origin of the name is so valuable

This address was presented as the annual Quaker Lecture at Western Yearly Meeting, in August of 1975.

that it ought to be better known than it is. The crucial passage is:

> Sometimes the Power of God will break forth into a whole meeting, and there will be such an inward travail while each is seeking to overcome the evil in themselves, that by the strong contrary workings of these opposite powers, like the going of two contrary tides, every individual will be strongly exercised, as in a day of battle, and thereby trembling; and a motion of body will be upon most, if not upon all, which, as the power of Truth prevails, will from pangs and groans end with a sweet sound of thanksgiving and praise, and from this the name of *Quakers*, i.e. *Tremblers*, was first reproachfully cast upon us, which, though it be none of our choosing, yet in this respect we are not ashamed of it, but have rather reason to rejoice therefore.

Though I have long been familiar with this noble passage it came to have a new significance for me earlier this summer when my wife and I were visiting Russian Christians. Often there would develop a buzzing sound as hundreds of the gathered company voiced their personal prayers in a semi-audible whisper. In Barclay's words, it was indeed "a sweet sound of thanksgiving and praise." Contemporary experience may thus shed light on ancient fact. As I listened to the Russian Christians, many of whom have suffered persecution as our own ancestors once did, I realized that they may be closer in spirit to the early Quakers than we are today in our comfortable and safe existence.

When Barclay and Penn, and others like them, decided to take a scornful term and glorify it, there had already been a history of possible names for the new movement. The Seekers who had become Finders in the North of England sometimes referred to themselves as "Children of the Light," sometimes as "Friends in the Truth," and often simply as "Friends." It must be understood, however, that these were not, in the first instance, looked upon as denominational labels, or as terms for which they had a monopoly. The titles, it was believed, belonged equally to all persons anywhere who had a living experience of Christ and who had become His emissaries in the world. The Biblical term "Children of the Light" (Ephesians 5:8) was adopted at first, not out of a spirit of self-adulation, but as an effort to report what had actually occurred. No one was able to say it better than Edward Burrough, whose memorable words are:

> Then began we to sing praises to the Lord God Almighty and
> to the Lamb forever, who had redeemed us to God, and brought
> us out of the captivity and bondage of the world, and put an end
> to sin and death, and all this was by and through and in the
> Light of Christ within us.

The Light of Christ, it was joyously believed, was actually
shining in each human heart, though many were unchanged
because they did not respond to it. The new message of George
Fox, after his illumination on Pendle Hill in the early summer
of 1652, was that Christ had come to teach His people Himself.
Many who heard this vibrant message, realized that they were
indeed His people and, because they were yoked with Him,
they were necessarily yoked with one another. The experience
of the indwelling Light of Christ led, consequently, to a new
sense of fellowship. It was the experience of fellowship which
led to the use of the term "Friends." Those who began to use
this term for themselves were influenced, in part, by Christ's
own usage when He said "I have called you friends" (John
15:15).

When we think carefully we soon realize that no single name
for a movement such as ours is ever satisfactory. Though the
word "Friends" has endured, it has always suffered from an
intrinsic ambiguity. The outsider asks "Friends of what or of
whom?" Indeed, there are many groups such as "Friends of
the Library" or "Friends of the Symphony" which increase the
confusion. When we include an adjective and say "Religious
Society of Friends" we add a measure of clarity, but the
language is still far from satisfactory. It says nothing about
the mission in the world, and, worst of all, it says nothing
about Christ. There is, therefore, no great surprise in the fact
that outsiders often fail to recognize that we are a Christian
body at all.

It is in the effort to solve the problems of ambiguity that
some of our members now employ more ecclesiastical language
and refer to "Friends Church." The serious danger of this
usage is that it indicates to the outsider that we think of
ourselves as being little more than another denominational
institution in the community. Perhaps that is what we
sometimes become, as matter of fact, but when that is true we

121

have already lost our vision and deserve to perish. It was not for such a mild version of Christianity that our ancestors suffered! Always the real heresy appears when we make small what Christ evidently meant to make large.

The chief reason why no single term for a Christian movement ever suffices is that there are so many sides to it. The fellowship, which we denote when we say "Friends" is one side, but it is not the only side. There is also the mission, and there is the ministry. We cannot think of a single word or phrase that can successfully include all phases adequately. If we are faithful to our vision of a great people to be gathered and sent forth, we must pay equal stress to three sides of the whole, the life of devotion, the life of service, and the life of the mind. In short, we are called, by Christ, to pray, to serve and to think, and if any one of the three is neglected the other two suffer accordingly.

Our search for identity is greatly aided by our acceptance of the wisdom of our best minds of three centuries ago, in thinking of ourselves not as a church, or a sect or a society, but as a "People." We are a people who know that we are called to keep alive in the world the vision of Basic Christianity. With all of our own incompetence and personal failure clearly recognized, we are trying to be loyal to the vision which Christ has given of a fellowship which, being committed to Christ, seeks consequently to penetrate the world. Such a movement is not merely a "meeting" since that would suggest that the gathering together is an end in itself; it must also be a "scattering." A people so committed necessarily seeks to penetrate business, education, labor, family life and even government. It was this conception of a "People" which made it natural for Robert Barclay to become Governor of what we call New Jersey and for William Penn to become the founder of Pennsylvania.

The path of wisdom seems to be that of adopting the world's scornful title and giving it such richness of connotation that we thereby remind ourselves of what our vision really is. We must engage in an agonizing reappraisal of what the vocation of the People called Quakers is and ought to be. This we can never answer adequately, but we can at least determine never to settle for anything small. We need to contemplate often the disturbing words of Christ, "Something greater than the temple is here" (Matthew 12:6).

As we encounter Christ's own vision of the people who would be committed to Him, we soon note how this vision surpassed that of either the temple or the synagogue. The temple was a place of ritual sacrifice and this Christ transcended radically. Those committed to Him understand very well that He does not require any ceremony at all. This is a witness still sorely needed in the world because of the constant temptation to substitute ritual for reality. There is need in the world for a people who can know and say clearly that without the reality no ceremony will suffice and that with the reality no ceremony is required. The reality is the real presence of Christ, humbling, lifting and enabling any person made in God's image.

A few weeks ago, in the Baptist meetinghouse of Moscow, my wife and I watched as nineteen men and women entered the visible fellowship by the act of immersion in water. We were impressed with the dedication represented, but we understood thoroughly that it was the dedication rather than the ceremony which was primary. When people asked me, as they often do, whether I had been baptized, I said I trusted that I had been, but I felt compelled to add that no ritual had been involved. I referred to the moving words of the Apostle Paul, "There is one body and one Spirit, just as you were called to the one hope that belongs to your call, one Lord, one faith, one baptism" (Ephesians 4:4, 5). I went on to point out that it is not conceivable that the "one baptism" is either that of immersion or sprinkling or any other outward ceremony, but is, instead, the real act of commitment to Christ which makes us members of His spiritual body.

Just as we are called to something far larger than any temple, which is essentially a shrine, so also we are called to something larger than the synagogue. We know that Christ attended the synagogue in Nazareth at a crucial point in His public ministry, but, if we follow the account provided by Mark, there is no indication that He ever attended again. Instead, he called His associates to Him, "and began to send them out" (Mark 6:7). Here is the real beginning of the Christian movement as something distinct from its spiritual predecessors. The characteristic preposition of both the

Temple and the Synagogue was "in," but the characteristic preposition of the new vision was "out." People came into the temple area or the synagogue as the end of a process, but Christ saw a possibility that was different in kind. He saw a spiritual movement characterized primarily by *mission*.

We understand better what it is that we are meant to be when we stress both mission and ministry, for *it is our mission to minister*. In May of this year, I spent many happy days in the Library of Friends House, London. Perhaps the happiest day of all was that in which I held in my hand and studied carefully a document which was written three hundred eighteen years ago, by Robert Fowler, the captain of the ship *Woodhouse*. Many of you know the central words of this document because they are deeply inscribed in the wooden beam which stands above the fireplace of the dining room of Earlham College. One day, twenty years ago, when Tom Jones and I were standing in the partly completed structure of the new Earlham Hall, we selected a sound beam of the old Earlham Hall, then being demolished, and decided to adorn it with Fowler's words, so that generations to come might thereby become familiar with them. The central passage, which I have recently read again in London, is "The ministers of Christ were not idle. They gathered sticks, and kindled a fire, and left it burning."

All of us will understand better the vision which possesses us if we know the mission of the *Woodhouse*. The challenging situation was that New England seemed to be closed to the Quaker mission. Any master of a ship found guilty of bringing Quakers into the Massachusetts Bay Colony was liable to a fine of one hundred pounds. In spite of this, and possibly because of this, a Quaker of Bridlington, Robert Fowler, decided to build a ship "in the cause of truth" and named it the *Woodhouse*. Though the ship seemed to be too small for the Atlantic crossing, Fowler felt that God was guiding him to offer the vessel for the voyage to New England. All who volunteered as Quaker passengers were well aware that they faced the clear prospect of death. In spite of this prospect, eleven persons, seven men and four women, volunteered to sail with Fowler from London. One of them, William Robinson, was actually hanged in Boston, as one of the four Boston martyrs. The eleven passengers were Christopher Holder, John Copeland, William Brent, Sarah Gibbons, Mary Wetherhead, Dorothy Waugh, William Robinson, Humphrey Norton, Richard Doudney, Robert Hodgson, and Mary Clark. The first six of these had been expelled from Boston earlier.

On the south coast of England the little ship anchored because of needed repairs. Instead of remaining on ship where they were useless, and thereby wasting valuable time, the eleven passengers went on shore, each trying to make contact with new seekers who might be drawn into the fellowship. It was of this action that the captain wrote so movingly when he began, "The ministers of Christ were not idle." This has become one of our most revealing stories during the three hundred twenty-five years of Quaker history. We must note what Fowler called these incendiary Christians. He did not call them Friends, or Children of the Light, or Quakers, but "ministers of Christ." Here is our noblest vision expressed in memorable words at one of the noblest points in our story.

Several of these people suffered severely. William Brent, the most elderly of the voyagers, was, in the summer of 1658, flogged almost to death, while Christopher Holder and John Copeland were the first to suffer the ear-cropping penalty. Because of difficult winds, the *Woodhouse* landed at New Amsterdam rather than in New England, but six of the "ministers of Christ" went on to the more dangerous area as soon as they could get there.

You and I are not likely to be flogged mercilessly, as was Robert Hodgson at New Amsterdam, but we can, at least, follow partially in his footsteps by seeing ourselves, whatever our other callings may be, as "ministers of Christ." This is our primary calling. We are not called to be observers of performances, but participants in a mission. Since it is not possible to be a Christian alone we must be part of a fellowship, not merely a Society of Friends, but, far more significantly, a "Society of Ministers." The word Quaker is a short-hand expression for this potent idea.

We understand clearly, of course, that we have no monopoly on this idea, since it is shared, in varying degrees, by others. When William Booth had his own vision of the nature of a Christian society one hundred ten years ago, he called his

125

group the Christian Mission. The first public meeting of this group, which later became known as the Salvation Army, was held in a tent set up in the Quaker burial ground at Bunhill Fields, London. Very early this mission involved both husbands and wives, and to this day no man can become an officer of the Salvation Army unless, in case he is a married man, his wife shares the responsibility with him. If they are not on mission they cannot be members.

Much of the vision which possesses us, the vision of a Society of Ministers in common life, is shared by the Latter Day Saints and Jehovah's Witnesses. In both of these, the conception of universal ministry is widely held and often better demonstrated than it is among ourselves. Whenever our vision is shared, it is reasonable that we should rejoice, since we seek a time when this dream permeates the entire Christian Movement.

The forms of ministry in which we can engage are legion. Like Margaret Fell, contemporary women can use their homes as centers in which Christian vitality is nourished. Margaret virtually made Swarthmoor Hall into a retreat center in which she ministered to other ministers. Once they had been revived, she sent them out to new efforts. One hundred fifty years later, the Gurneys made Earlham Hall into another renewal house, in which various Christian movements were inaugurated and encouraged. In our own fashion and within the limits of our strength, we can do the same today.

One hundred years ago, our grandparents started a new chapter by establishing the pastoral system, thereby saving many congregations from almost certain death. They recognized that they were afflicted with a serious sickness, the essence of which was a widespread lack of ministry of all kinds. They moved, accordingly, from very little ministry to what soon became a professional ministry. Now, as we approach the end of the twentieth century, we have an opportunity to take an even greater step, to move from a professional ministry to a total ministry, shared by both women and men in common life.

The vision of Basic Christianity which possesses us is one in which a Christian unit is like a symphony orchestra, in which there are many kinds of instruments, but in which every one, including the smallest, is needed for the total production.

Some ought to travel in the ministry, but others ought to stay at home. Some ought to write books, but others ought to help in their distribution. What books are you distributing to seekers these days? Often you can bring a real change in some life by handing a book to some person and saying simply, "This has spoken to me. Would you like to see if it can speak to you?"

The opportunities for those who see themselves as ministers of Christ are indeed numerous. It is a serious mistake to suppose that ministry is limited to public speaking, since there are so many other ways of gathering sticks and kindling fires. Here is where the language of the *Woodhouse* captain is helpful to us today, after a lapse of more than three hundred years. For many of us the chief form of the ministry is more that of Barnabas than that of Paul. Barnabas did not write even one of the New Testament books, while Paul wrote many, but the important truth is that, apart from the modest work of Barnabas, Paul would not have written at all. It was Barnabas who hunted for the gifted man and brought him into his amazing usefulness (Acts 11:25). It was not for nothing that this humble Christian was nicknamed, "Son of Encouragement" (Acts 4:36).

It is right that some should travel in the ministry, but it is also right that others should help to support financially those who serve in this fashion. During May of this year, there was an exhibit in Friends House, London, which explained the origin of the "Kendal Fund." This fund, even before the voyage of the *Woodhouse,* was organized by Margaret Fell to assist travellers, including those known as "The Valiant Sixty." Some of the Boston martyrs, obviously unable to defray their own travel expenses, were aided in this fashion. Now, as then, one valuable form of ministry is the ministry of money. Money is potentially holy because of what can be accomplished by it.

One significant aspect of the larger ministry, as Friends at their best have envisioned it, is that it is something from which no one can ever retire. In one sense, I retired nine years ago. By this it is meant that in 1966, I ceased to be Professor of Philosophy at Earlham, but, of course, I did not retire from the ministry. How *could* I? You can retire from an appointment, but you cannot retire from a commitment! Once the vision really possesses a person it determines his conduct to the last day of his life. This is the controlling idea which has given a certain unity to all of the various chapters of my life.

I greet you today, therefore, as fellow-ministers. I entreat you to ask, over and over, "In what ministry am I engaged?" You may not hold the log of the *Woodhouse* in your own hands, but you can ask where you are gathering sticks and kindling some fire that, apart from your labor, would not be burning.

Each one of us is keenly aware of his own unworthiness when measured by this standard. We are not, at this point in history, a Society of Ministers of Christ, but that is not the end of the matter. There is something worse than personal failure, and that is the loss of the standard. The vision is really our greatest asset, because, without it, we are not even aware of our failures. Therefore we must cherish the vision, telling of it over and over as we mingle with one another. Underlying all of our meetings, all of our committees, all of our building programs, all of our travels, is the vision of a fellowship which gathers in order to scatter and which worships in order to serve. It is to the perpetuation, the implementation and the embodiment of this vision that we are committed.